AF691544

Luke Wilcox is one of the leading rating practitioners in the country. He has appeared four times in the Supreme Court, and in many of the most significant valuation cases of the last decade. He advises and acts for clients from multinational corporations to central government departments, and regularly lectures at national rating events. His expertise in the field was recognised in 2024, when he was elected as an honorary member of the Rating Surveyors' Association. His valuation practice is not limited to rating, and he is experienced in valuation disputes in compulsory purchase compensation, rent review, lease renewals, and other property-based taxes. He is a member of Landmark Chambers, where in addition to rating and valuation he practices in planning, environmental, and property law.

A Practical Guide to Valuation for Rating

A Practical Guide to Valuation for Rating

Luke Wilcox MA (Oxon)
Barrister at Law (Middle Temple)

Law Brief Publishing

© Luke Wilcox

All rights reserved. No part of this publication may be reproduced, stored in a retrieval system, or transmitted, in any form or by any means, electronic, mechanical, photocopying, recording or otherwise, without the prior permission of the publisher.

Excerpts from judgments and statutes are Crown copyright. Any Crown Copyright material is reproduced with the permission of the Controller of OPSI and the King's Printer for Scotland. Some quotations may be licensed under the terms of the Open Government Licence (http://www.nationalarchives.gov.uk/doc/open-government-licence/version/3).

Cover image © iStockphoto.com/coldsnowstorm

The information in this book was believed to be correct at the time of writing. All content is for information purposes only and is not intended as legal advice. No liability is accepted by either the publisher or author for any errors or omissions (whether negligent or not) that it may contain. Professional advice should always be obtained before applying any information to particular circumstances.

Published 2024 by Law Brief Publishing, an imprint of Law Brief Publishing Ltd
30 The Parks
Minehead
Somerset
TA24 8BT

www.lawbriefpublishing.com

Paperback: 978-1-916698-49-9

For Dan Kolinsky KC,

the model of a rating specialist at the Bar,

for teaching me how it's done

PREFACE

The law of rating is ancient.

It was first established on a national basis[1] by the Poor Relief Act of 1601, though aspects of the system existed even earlier. The concept of the "hereditament" as the basic unit of property in respect of which liability arises was codified by the Parochial Assessments Act 1836, and the notion of valuation lists containing the details of the valuation of hereditaments goes back to the Rating and Valuation Act 1925. It is the oldest tax in continuous existence in the UK.[2]

The modern law of rating is found in the Local Government Finance Act 1988 ("the 1988 Act"), and its associated secondary legislation. While this statutory machinery is only a few decades old, the key concepts on which it is based have been refined over centuries of professional and judicial consideration. That is a process which continues today: fundamental issues like the character of the hereditament and the identification of the rateable occupier have been litigated at the highest level in the last ten years, and continue to generate controversy.

That litigation is driven by its financial importance to those affected by it. Rating accounts for tens of billions of pounds of local authority revenue every year, and is for many businesses one of their largest outgoings.

As a tax on the occupation and ownership of property, the quantum of rating liability is dictated primarily by the value of the property in question. The valuation of property for rating purposes is thus at the heart of many rating disputes, and is a subtle and established field in its

---

1 In England at least – the law of rating is older than the UK, or even the Union of the English and Scottish Crowns.

2 *Woolway (VO) v Mazars* [2015] AC 1862.

own right. There are no fewer than three professional organisations active in the field: the Royal Institution of Chartered Surveyors (a body so venerable that its headquarters is on Parliament Square, next door to the UK Supreme Court); the Institute of Revenues, Rating and Valuation; and the Rating Surveyors' Association, a specialist rating body which was founded as long ago as 1909. Rating valuation is an art and a science, and there is a large corpus of professional learning which informs rating surveyors' approaches to their tasks. As with any profession of this kind, rating surveying has developed a language of its own, and proceeds on the basis of many assumptions and implicit understandings which can seem opaque to the uninitiated.

This, then, is a field both subtle and arcane, with a vast body of jurisprudence and professional guidance to understand, an established profession dedicated to its practice, and large amounts of client money at stake.

It is no surprise, therefore, that rating can be a daunting field for lawyers.

The purpose of this book is to help lawyers (and, I hope, anyone else with an interest in the subject) to understand how they can best contribute to disputes around rating valuation.

There are, broadly, two ways in which the lawyer can contribute.

The first is by assisting rating surveyors in understanding the legal parameters of the valuation exercise they are to undertake. The second is through assisting with the preparation and testing of evidence in rating challenges and appeals.

Those two functions have informed the structure of this book.

Part 1 looks at the legal framework for identifying what it is, exactly, that the rating surveyor is required to value. What is the ambit of the property, and what are its characteristics? What assumptions are to be made about the property market, and who is doing the bidding for the property in that market? Put another way, what, precisely, is the question that the valuer is being asked to answer? These and related questions will be considered.

Part 2 seeks to give the lawyer a basic grasp of how rating surveyors approach the task of valuing property. What are the methods available, and how do they work? How are the methods selected, and what are the common strengths and weaknesses of each?

A book of this size cannot hope to treat these issues comprehensively, and I have not tried to cover every aspect of the subject. Rather, I have sought to give lawyers a solid grounding in the issues and language of rating, as a springboard for further research and discussion, and to enable lawyers to work with and add value to the client's professional surveying team. I have focused on the most recent authorities to deal with a subject (though reference to the classic old cases is both unavoidable and desirable), and at times I have tentatively given my own thoughts on the "hot topics" in the field. In places, I have ventured more detail and analysis on what may appear to be a small subject: where this is the case, it is, unashamedly, the result of my own academic interest in the nuance of that topic. Key terms which lawyers will need to know, and which they will hear in discussions with rating specialists, are in bold.

I hope that this book will be of assistance to anyone seeking to make their way into this fascinating branch of the law.

The law is stated as at 1 August 2024. This book deals with the law of England: while the principles of valuation apply equally in Wales (and indeed in many other jurisdictions), some of the procedures around rating valuation appeals differ slightly between the jurisdictions. Any errors are my own.

Luke Wilcox
August 2024

CONTENTS

PART ONE THE RATING HYPOTHESIS

Chapter One What Is the Thing to Be Valued? 3

Chapter Two The Hereditament and the Hypothetical Tenancy 9

Chapter Three The Statutory Assumptions 19

Chapter Four The Relevant Dates 31

Chapter Five The Circumstances of the Property and Its Locality 35

PART TWO VALUATION

Chapter Six Valuation Methodologies and Their Selection 49

Chapter Seven The Rentals Method 55

Chapter Eight Comparable Assessments and the Tone of the List 71

Chapter Nine The Receipts and Expenditure Method 79

Chapter Ten The Contractor's Basis of Valuation 99

Chapter Eleven Other Methods 113

PART ONE

THE RATING HYPOTHESIS

CHAPTER ONE

WHAT IS THE THING TO BE VALUED?

Before a property (or indeed anything else) can be valued, it is first necessary to define with sufficient precision the thing which is to be valued, and the circumstances in which it is to be valued: there is no such thing as a valuation "at large". Unless and until the nature of the subject property is properly understood, the valuer's expert judgment cannot be applied.

The identification of the character and parameters of the subject property is not, itself, a matter of valuation judgment (though some components of the subject may require expert opinion to define). Rather, the exercise is one which involves the interpretation of the statutory regime and the jurisprudence, and extensive legal analysis. This is one of the key areas where legal advice is sought and provided in the rating valuation field.

Broadly speaking, there are three stages to the process of definition which must be undertaken before the valuation can be attempted.

a. Identifying the property to be valued. It is generally convenient to talk and think about the valuation of property or land as though the property or the land itself were a thing of value. Strictly speaking, however, that is not the case: in England and Wales, no private person directly owns any land at all. What people actually own, and the thing that property valuers are actually concerned with, are rights over land. Such rights range from very extensive proprietary estates, such as freeholds or long leaseholds, to heritable but non-possessory rights like easements or *profits a prendre*, to personal rights such as contractual licences. In all cases, the content and character of the package of rights which makes up the "property" is critical to its value. An unencumbered freehold estate over an area of land, for instance, will clearly have a different value to a one-year non-exclusive licence over the same area. Equally, the particular rights in the package will almost always be accompanied by a series of obligations on the holder of the rights: a freeholder's estate over a field may be subject to an obligation not to obstruct a neighbouring landowner's right of way across the field, for instance. Similarly, a tenant of an office may be subject to obligations to maintain the property in a certain state. And anyone with an occupational right over land is subject to limitations imposed by the planning regime: the freeholder of a field does not, by virtue of that freehold, have the right to build a tower on the field unless he[1] first obtains planning permission. For rating purposes, the particular package of rights and obligations which make up the subject of the valuation is defined by the 1988 Act, and is known as the "**hereditament**".

b. Identifying the time at which the property is to be valued. Once the package of rights and obligations which make up the property are identified and defined, it is then necessary to identify the particular date at which the property valuation is to occur. That date is of considerable significance: the property market, like most markets, is in a state of almost constant flux, so that a difference of even a few weeks in the valuation date can affect the price to be paid. Similarly, knowledge about the market fluctuates as well: if an economic actor becomes aware of relevant data about the property or the market on a given day, then the price he would be willing to pay for the property on that day may be very different to that which he would have been willing to pay the day before. The property and its locality will also vary over time: the closure of the anchor store in a shopping mall has a

1 Throughout this book, masculine pronouns should be read as including the feminine and (where appropriate) the neuter or plural.

significant impact on values of other units in the mall, for instance. Legal status is relevant here too: a change in the planning status of the property can have a dramatic impact on its value. In the rating context, there are two relevant dates which need to be considered: the **valuation date**, which is the date on which the package of rights and obligations comprising the property is assumed to come into existence; and the **material day**, which is the date on which a series of specified features of the property (such as its physical state and the occupation of other premises in the locality) are fixed. The statutory machinery is set up in such a way that, for any given valuation, the valuation date and the material day are never the same: the result is that a degree of expert judgment (and no small amount of imagination) is required to transpose the material day factors to the valuation date.

c. Identifying the circumstances appliable at the relevant date. Once the property is identified and the relevant dates confirmed, the final part of the exercise is to identify the facts applicable to the property at those dates. This is mostly a factual exercise. However, it is not uncommon for issues both of law and expert judgment to arise at this stage as well. What amounts to a "matter affecting the physical enjoyment" of a property, for instance, is an issue on which legal input is usually required; and the extent of the area which amounts to the "locality" of a property can require expert opinion as to the nature of the businesses conducted for properties in the relevant mode or category of occupation.

Once those three issues are addressed, the valuer is able to proceed with the valuation of the property.

In the specific context of non-domestic rating, the set of legal principles which govern these three definitional issues is usually referred to as the "**rating hypothesis**" or the "**statutory hypothesis**".

The principles emanate principally from Schedule 6 to the 1988 Act; but Sch 6 is impossible to understand or apply without reference to the extensive body of rating case law which has developed over many decades, and which considerably pre-dates the 1988 Act itself. Indeed, so extensive and cohesive is the body of case law in this field that it has been referred to as "*the 'common law' of rating*" (*Williams (VO) v Scottish and Newcastle Retail Ltd* [2001] RA 41 at para 54).

Rating appeals and procedures

Before considering these issues, it is worth saying something about the tribunal structure applicable to rating valuation, and the procedure by which parties can bring disputes before the tribunals. This is governed by the Non-Domestic Rating (Alteration of Lists and Appeals) (England) Regulations 2009, as amended. In England, the name for the procedure established by the current iteration of these regulations is "**check challenge appeal**", or "CCA". As the name suggests, this involves three stages, which, in brief summary, are as follows:

a. The first stage requires the ratepayer[2] to provide the VO with information about the property, and to confirm the accuracy of the information which the VO already holds, so that the VO can check the accuracy of the list entry.

b. Following the completion of a check, it is open to the ratepayer to make a formal challenge to the accuracy of the rating list, by making a **proposal** for the alteration of the list. The grounds on which a proposal can be made are specified in reg 4 of the 2009 regulations. While the CCA process itself has only been in place since 2017, the use of proposals as the vehicle for challenging the

2 There are a range of other persons who are also able to trigger this procedure, if they meet the regulatory definition of an "interested party": reg 2.

content of the rating list has been in place throughout the life of the 1988 Act. On receipt of a proposal, the VO can make the change sought; can make some other change to the list, if agreed by all relevant parties (as specified in reg 12); or the VO can decline to make any alteration.

c. If no alteration is made, because the VO regards the proposal as not well-founded, then the ratepayer has an automatic right of appeal to the Valuation Tribunal for England ("VTE"), a specialist tribunal which deals with disputes around the contents of the rating lists, as well as the valuation lists prepared for the Council Tax. Appeals against decisions of the VTE lie to the Upper Tribunal (Lands Chamber), a specialist tribunal which is constituted of senior lawyers as well as very experienced surveyors and valuers. Unusually, the Upper Tribunal hears appeals on a *de novo* basis, so the parties are able to call fresh evidence and advance new arguments, and the Upper Tribunal will make its own findings of fact afresh, rather than reviewing the VTE's findings. There is no permission to appeal mechanism for either tribunal, and in important cases it is almost guaranteed that the relevant tribunal of fact will end up being the Upper Tribunal. Onward appeal lies from the Upper Tribunal, on points of law only, to the Court of Appeal and the Supreme Court.

Lord Carnwath JSC made important observations about the function of this appeal system in *Cardtronics UK Ltd v Sykes (VO)* [2020] 1 WLR 2184 at para 4:

> *"It is important however to be clear where lies the primary responsibility for reviewing the valuation officer's decisions. Although the first appeal is to the Valuation Tribunal, and the Upper Tribunal acts as an appellate body, it does so by way of a full rehearing, not simply review, if necessary hearing evidence for that purpose … By contrast, onward appeal to the Court of Appeal lies only on points of law. Accordingly, it is to the Upper*

> *Tribunal's judgment that we must look first for the relevant findings of fact and their evaluation. To justify intervention at a higher level it is necessary to identify something more than a difference of evaluative assessment. Further in this highly specialised area of the law the higher courts should give particular weight to the expertise which has been developed by the senior judges and members of the Upper Tribunal (Lands Chamber)."*

We now turn to consider in detail the components of the statutory hypothesis.

CHAPTER TWO

THE HEREDITAMENT AND THE HYPOTHETICAL TENANCY

The heart of the rating hypothesis is found in para 2(1) of Sch 6 to the 1988 Act, which provides as follows:

> *"The rateable value of a non-domestic hereditament none of which consists of domestic property and none of which is exempt from local non domestic rating shall be taken to be an amount equal to the rent at which it is estimated the hereditament might reasonably be expected to let from year to year"*

That basic formulation is subject to three assumptions, which will be explored below. First, though, it is worth considering some of the components of the basic formulation.

"The hereditament"

An entire textbook could be written on the subtleties of the concept of the hereditament in rating law. For the purposes of a textbook on valuation, however, it is sufficient to note that the hereditament is the term for the unit of property[3] in respect of which the hypothetical tenancy arises.

---

[3] There are some instances in which the hereditament does not comprise physical property at all, but rather consists of rights over other physical property. A right to display an advertisement, for instance, can in some cases be an incorporeal hereditament separate from the physical property over

As to the extent of that unit of property, s. 64(1) of the 1988 Act defines it by reference to the definition contained in s. 115 of the old General Rate Act 1967. The s. 115 definition was as follows:

> *""hereditament" means property which is or may become liable to a rate, being a unit of such property which is, or would fall to be, shown as a separate item in the valuation list"*

The circularity of that definition has been noticed by the judiciary. In the leading case of *Woolway (VO) v Mazars LLP* [2015] AC 1862, Lord Sumption JSC observed that "*the meaning of "hereditament" is left to be elucidated by the courts in accordance with the principles underlying the rating Acts.*" Somewhat less euphemistically, in *Reeves (VO) v Northrop* [2013] 1 WLR 2867 the Court of Appeal noted in respect of the statutory definition that "*if prizes are to be offered for legislative gobbledegook then the foregoing would surely qualify*" (para 9).

In the author's opinion, the statutory definition is not entirely unhelpful. It should be noted in particular that it concerns property which is or may become liable to a rate, singular. The concept of "a rate" is inextricably linked to the occupation of land, since it is the occupier[4] who is rateable, not the land (*Westminster CC v Southern Railway Co* [1936] AC 511 per Lord Russell of Killowen at 529). Since it is a person who is liable to a rate, and since a rate is levied on a person and not on property, it follows that a hereditament can only ever have a single owner or occupier.[5] The hereditament can thus be understood as property in a single person's

---

which the right exists: s. 64(2) of the 1988 Act. The same is true for the right to use land to operate a utilities meter (s. 64(3)). Those highly specialist hereditaments are beyond the scope of this book.

4 And in the case of unoccupied property, the owner: s. 45 of the 1988 Act.

5 The Courts have confirmed this principle: see for instance *R (Curzon Berkeley) v Bliss (VO)* [2002] RA 45 at para 54.

occupation, the value of which determines[6] the quantum of that person's liability.

It does not follow, however, that all of the land a person occupies comprises a single hereditament. In *Mazars*, which concerned two non-contiguous floors of an office building, in the common occupation of Mazars, the Supreme Court identified two main tests which determine how many hereditaments are contained in any given occupier's property holdings (para 12):

a. The primary test is known as the **geographical test**, and is concerned with visual or cartographic unity. If property is self-contained, in the sense that any part of it can be reached from any other part without going on to property of which the occupier is not in occupation, then it is probably a single hereditament. Conversely, if you have to go on to third party property (such as a landlord's retained common parts, or a public highway) to get from one part of the property to another part, then the parts are probably two hereditaments. Whether or not any given means of intercommunication is sufficient to unify two areas of property for the purposes of the geographical test is sensitive to the physical nature of the properties themselves: *F C Brown Steel Equipment Ltd v Hopkins (VO)* [2022] UKUT 51 (LC).[7]

---

6 At least *prima facie*: there are a wide range of other factors which affect the amount of rates a person is actually liable to pay, including the modifiers set by central government, and the application of the range of mandatory and discretionary reliefs available to certain occupiers of certain properties. Those are not, however, valuation issues at all, and nothing more will be said about them here.

7 The Rating (Property in Common Occupation) and Council Tax (Empty Dwellings) Act 2018 has modified the geographical principle in England, so that in some cases, contiguous but non-interconnecting properties are treated as one hereditament rather than as two. This followed professional

A necessary implication of the geographical test is that, in order to be a hereditament, the extent of the property must be capable of being defined with sufficient clarity. Where the extent of a person's occupation is nebulous, so that the boundaries of the occupied land cannot be clearly identified, then the property may be incapable of being a hereditament at all. In *Cardtronics UK Ltd v Sykes (VO)* [2020] 1 WLR 2184, for instance, the sites of a number of cash machines were incapable of being hereditaments, because their essential qualities were those of impermanence and mobility (para 39, per Lord Carnwath of Notting Hill JSC).

b. The secondary test is called the **functional test**. Where two areas of property in common occupation are geographically separate, they can nevertheless be treated as a single hereditament if, on an objective assessment, the use of one is necessary to the effectual enjoyment of the other, so that the two parts could not reasonably be separately let. A classic example is a golf course bisected by a public footpath. The footpath, being a highway, prevents the two parts of the course from being geographically unified; but no-one would let half a golf course without also letting the other half, so the functional test treats the geographically separate parts as a single hereditament. Conversely, if discrete parts of a geographically unified area of property are used for wholly different purposes, the functional test can split the self-contained property into two hereditaments. The example given in *Mazars* is of a factory within the curtilage of a residence (para 6). The Supreme Court stressed that the functional test us to be applied objectively, by reference to the ascertainable character of the properties themselves, rather than by reference to the subjective business needs of the occupier.

---

and media concern about the implications of the geographical principle for small businesses.

"Let from year to year"

This part of the hypothesis prescribes the nature of the property interest which the valuer is to value: a tenancy from year to year.

The concept of a tenancy is one which is readily understandable to an English lawyer. What is less obvious is the nature of a tenancy "from year to year". The Courts have held that the concept envisaged is that of an annual tenancy, but one in which the tenant has a reasonable prospect of continuing his tenancy beyond any given year.

There are a number of judicial expressions of this notion; perhaps the clearest is that of Lord Wilberforce in the leading rating case of *Dawkins v Ash Brothers and Heaton Ltd* [1969] 2 AC 366 at 387:

> *"we should regard the words "from year to year" as meaning no more than that the tenancy is not a fixed or definite one; it is one of indefinite duration, determinable by notice, but not, I would think, according to the technicalities governing the giving of notice in tenancies of this kind. What then, are we to say of the tenant's expectations and of the rent he is consequently willing to pay? I see no reason why, if there is evidence to prove it, a greater and more reliable expectation of continuance should not be allowed to affect his calculation."*

In the same appeal, Lord Pearson described the tenancy as "*a normal tenancy from year to year running on indefinitely until terminated by notice*" (391).

While the tenancy is assumed to have a reasonable prospect of continuance, the valuer plainly does not proceed on the basis that the tenancy will in fact continue forever – that would be to transform the tenancy into a de facto freehold. The correct approach was explained by the Hong Kong Court of Appeal[8] in *China Light and Power Co Ltd v Commissioner of Rating and Valuation* [1996] RA 475 by Godfrey JA at 534 in these terms:

> *"It is legitimate, in my judgement, to base the valuation on the footing of a reasonable prospect of the hypothetical tenant continuing to be a tenant, not simply in the abstract, but for some reasonable period of time, and I can see nothing wrong with the Lands Tribunal, as part of the process of valuation, making an assumption as to the duration of that reasonable period of time. It would not be legitimate for the Lands Tribunal to value the tenements on the footing that the hypothetical tenant had a term of, say "X" years certain. But it would be legitimate for the lands Tribunal to value the tenements on the footing of a tenancy from year to year, with a reasonable prospect that the tenancy would in fact continue for "X" years."*

That approach was agreed by the Upper Tribunal in *Hardman (VO) v British Gas Trading Ltd* [2015] RA 254 at para 149. The Tribunal summarised the effect of the law in this way (para 158):

> *"the concept of the hypothetical tenancy as a tenancy from year to year but one with an indefinite prospect of continuance, requires the valuer (and if necessary this Tribunal on appeal) to consider, in the light of all the facts and circumstances, what probable length of time the hypothetical landlord and the hypothetical tenant would attribute to that prospect of continuance. In our judgement it is wrong as a matter of law to suppose that the possibility of a rent review must prevent the hypothetical parties from contemplating continuance much*

8 The Hong Kong rating system is closely modelled on the English one, and the case law of the Hong Kong courts and tribunals is often of considerable assistance in understanding the English regime.

> *beyond two years. It is also wrong, to put the point in a slightly different way, to say that the consequence of valuing the hypothetical tenancy on the basis of continuance for some or possibly many years is implicitly to convert a tenancy from year to year into a tenancy for a term of years. The correct approach requires the valuer to consider all the facts and circumstances that relate to the hereditament in order to judge what sort of length in terms of a prospect of continuance would be appropriate in that particular case. In the case of some forms of hereditament the exercise may be perfectly straightforward and the prospect of continuance may have little or no role to play in the valuation. In the case of hereditaments that involve a considerable initial investment, such as canals and railways in the old cases and power stations in modern times, the facts and circumstances may well provide powerful evidence upon which the valuer will conclude that the hypothetical parties would contemplate a tenancy from year to year with a lengthy prospect of continuance."*

In practice, valuers usually determine how long a reasonable prospect of continuance may be in any given case by looking at standard market practice for properties of the kind under consideration. In the office context, for instance, it is usual for the valuer to assume that the tenancy under the hypothesis will last as long as the real-world tenancies which form the evidence base for the valuation. The duration of those real-world tenancies is for these purposes measured either to the end of the lease or to the first break clause, whichever is sooner. In the sectors which do not generate real-world lettings, and where the valuer must adopt valuation methods which are not based on market practice, matters such as the rate of return on capital investments will become more important to this analysis. These are, however, all matters of valuer judgment, rather than issues of law.

"Might reasonably be expected to let"

The rating hypothesis makes clear, through the use of the word "reasonably", that the tenancy to be valued is not the actual tenancy of the actual occupier (if such a thing exists). Rather, what is envisaged is a **hypothetical tenancy** executed between hypothetical parties.

There is a plethora of authority on the character of the parties to the hypothetical tenancy. Perhaps the key characteristic is that the **hypothetical tenant** is willing to take a lease of the property on the statutory terms, and the **hypothetical landlord** is willing to let it on the same terms (*Smith v Churchwardens and Overseers of the Poor of the Parish of Birmingham* (1888) 22 QBD 211 per Wills J at 219). The valuer must therefore proceed on the basis that the hypothetical parties will arrive at a deal for the letting of the property on the statutory terms.

Furthermore, the hypothetical parties behave in a reasonable and prudent way in their dealings with one another. As Holgate J explained in *Hughes (VO) v Exeter City Council* [2020] RA 129 at para 36:

> *"it remains correct to regard the hypothetical landlord as an abstraction, an anonymous but reasonable person who goes about the letting as a prudent man of business, without giving the impression of being either over-anxious or unduly reluctant. Likewise, it should be assumed that the hypothetical tenant behaves reasonably, making proper enquiries about the property, and not appearing too anxious to take the letting."*

It is important to recall that, while the actual occupier or owner is not necessarily the hypothetical tenant, he is included in the pool of possible tenants for the hereditament under consideration (*LCC v Erith Parish Churchwardens* [1893] AC 562 per Lord Herschell LC at 588). Circumstances can arise where the actual occupier is the most likely person to make a successful bid for the property, because of real-world factors which must be taken into account (these are discussed later). Indeed, in some cases the actual occupier is the only person who would consider making a bid. In such cases the hypothetical tenant will have the characteristics of the actual occupier.

A good example of such a set of circumstances arose in *Celsa Steel (UK) Ltd v Webb (VO)* [2017] RA 143, which concerned a melt shop and rolling mill for the production of steel billet. The actual occupier of the steel mill was also the actual occupier and operator of another steel mill, located a mile away and joined to the subject property by a rail link. Such paired works are common in the real world, and there were no real-world examples of such paired mills having different operators. The two steel mills were separate hereditaments, and in valuing the first one, the principle of reality required the valuer to assume that the second one was occupied by its actual occupier (see further below). The result was that the actual occupier was the hypothetical tenant of the first mill: no-one other than the actual occupier would consider making a bid for one half of an integrated pair of sites.

The valuer's task is to judge the rent which the hypothetical parties would agree, given the real-world market conditions which existed at the valuation date. The competing interests of the parties, and the nature of the real-world competition in terms of both supply and demand, is usually referred to by rating surveyors as the "***higgling of the market***" (*Robinson Bros (Brewers) Ltd v Houghton and Chester-le-Street Assessment Committee* [1937] KB 445 per Scott LJ at 470).

In assessing supply and demand, the valuer is concerned with "general demand" for the property. It is not the case, therefore, that a saturated market will result in a low or nominal valuation for a property, even if in the real world the result of the market saturation is that there would be no demand for the property at all. Such an approach would undermine the purpose of rating valuation as providing a fair and equitable basis for assessing the tax liabilities of property occupiers and owners. Even in a saturated market, the rating hypothesis still assumes a willing landlord and a wiling tenant, and evidence derived from rental values for similar properties can provide the reference point for the hypothetical tenant's bid in such a case (*Hewitt (VO) v Telereal Trillium Ltd* [2019] 1 WLR 3262). *Telereal Trillium* drew a distinction, in this regard, between properties which were unoccupied because of a surplus of supply in the market, and properties which were unoccupied because they had become either technologically or economically obsolete. A "general demand" valuation is appropriate for the former type of property, but not for the latter.

CHAPTER THREE

THE STATUTORY ASSUMPTIONS

Para 2 of Sch 6 to the 1988 Act imposes requires the valuer to make three assumptions about the hypothetical tenancy which is being valued:

> *"(a) the first assumption is that the tenancy begins on the day by reference to which the determination is to be made;*
>
> *(b) the second assumption is that immediately before the tenancy begins the hereditament is in a state of reasonable repair, but excluding from this assumption any repairs which a reasonable landlord would consider uneconomic;*
>
> *(c) the third assumption is that the tenant undertakes to pay all usual tenant's rates and taxes and to bear the cost of the repairs and insurance and the other expenses (if any) necessary to maintain the hereditament in a state to command the rent mentioned above."*

Each of these assumptions raises issues for the valuer, and indeed for the legal adviser, to consider carefully in framing the valuation exercise.

The date the tenancy begins

The first assumption concerns the commencement date of the hypothetical tenancy. The statute requires the tenancy to be assumed to commence on "*the day by reference to which the determination is to be made*". That somewhat unhelpful language is explained by para 2(3) of

Sch 6 to be either (a) the day on which a rating list is compiled,[9] or (b) some earlier date specified by the Secretary of State by order.

In practice, the Secretary of State has, for every rating list since 1990, specified an earlier date under para 2(3). The specified date has always been the day two years before the date of compilation of any given rating list: thus the specified date for the current rating list, which was compiled on 1 April 2023, is 1 April 2021. The specified date is referred to by rating practitioners as the "**antecedent valuation date**" or AVD.

There are two main implications of the first statutory assumption.

The first is that the nature of the market in which the hypothetical parties "higgle" is that which existed on the AVD. If the AVD happens to fall at a time when the market is particularly strong, and if the market subsequently falls, then ratepayers can be saddled with RVs which are not reflective of the economic conditions in which the rates actually have to be paid. This occurred with particular severity with the 2010 List: the AVD for the 2010 list was 1 April 2008, which fell just before the global financial crisis which culminated in the collapse of Lehman Brothers in September 2008. By the time the 2010 List was compiled on 1 April 2010, the English and Welsh property markets were largely unrecognisable from those which had existed on 1 April 2008; yet

---

9 The "rating list" is a list, prepared by the statutory Valuation Officer ("VO"), for the area of each local authority (which for rating purposes is called a "billing authority"). There is also a "central valuation list", which is used for prescribed properties, or the properties of prescribed occupier, which tend to spread across multiple billing authority areas. Since 1990, the norm has been for a new set of rating lists to be compiled every five years, on 1 April. The 2010 rating list, however, lasted for seven years, and the 2017 list lasted for six years. The Non-Domestic Rating Act 2023 has reduced the standard duration of rating lists from five years to three years, so the current (2023) rating lists will be replaced by new lists on 1 April 2026.

ratepayers' RVs were based on pre-crisis levels of market supply and demand until March 2017.

Conversely, the current, 2023 List, has an AVD of 1 April 2021, which was during the COVID 19 pandemic. The result is that for a number of market sectors, RVs are based on considerably lower rents than those which their properties would currently demand.

The unfairnesses which result from such a state of affairs, both to ratepayers and to billing authorities, are obvious. Those unfairnesses will be mitigated somewhat by the passage of the Non-Domestic Rating Act 2023, section 5 of which increased the frequency of revaluations from every five years to every three years.

The second implication of the first statutory assumption is that the hypothetical parties' state of knowledge of market conditions is fixed as at the AVD. The hypothetical parties do not know anything which would not have been known to real-world actors on that date.

That is a simple enough principle. There are, however, three areas in which it can give rise to confusion, and which require clarification:

a. While valuers cannot treat the hypothetical parties as having post-AVD knowledge, valuers can take into account any future projections or predictions which a reasonable person in the hypothetical tenant's position might have formed on the basis of what was known at the AVD. As Lord Wilberforce put it in *Dawkins*, "*the hypothetical tenant is [not] so inescapably imprisoned in the present that no anticipation is permitted of what is to come*" (386).

b. While the hypothetical parties cannot be treated as knowing post-AVD facts, the principle does not prevent the valuer from taking into account post-AVD material in forming his view as to the hereditament's RV on the AVD. If, for example, a closely comparable property to the subject hereditament was actually let in the real world, on terms similar to those of the rating hypothesis, on 2 April 2021, the valuer is perfectly entitled, and indeed almost certainly required, to give considerable weight to that letting as evidence of the hereditament's RV for the 2023 list.

c. It is sometimes suggested that it is permissible to use hindsight to confirm the hypothetical parties' perceptions of trends which may have existed at the AVD. The jurisprudential foundation of that suggestion is the decision of the Hong Kong Lands Tribunal in *China Light and Power Co v Commissioner for Rating and Valuation* [1996] RA 475, where the Tribunal actively encouraged the use of post-valuation date accounts data in a receipts and expenditure valuation, on the basis that there was no reason to rely on what the hypothetical parties' conjecture would have been when the actual figures were known. The Tribunal proceeded on the basis that there is no bar in the rating regime on the use of hindsight, and cited *Bwllfa and Mrthyr Dare Steam Collieries (1891) Ltd v Pontypridd Waterworks Co* [1903] AC 426 as supporting authority. In the author's opinion, considerable care needs to be taken with that line of reasoning. The Tribunal did not cite the observation in *Bwllfa* by Lord Mcnaghten, at 431, that in the context of the statute[10] there under consideration "*I cannot find in [the Act] any provision or even suggestion to that effect that a line is to be drawn at the date of the counter-notice, and that all that happens after that date is to be as if it had never happened*". In the context of rating and the 1988 Act, however, the first statutory assumption in the rating hypothesis provides such a provision: to treat the hypothetical parties as being aware of post-AVD material is to undermine the assumption that their deal was concluded and executed on the AVD itself.

[10] Specifically, the Waterworks Clauses Act 1847

A point which is related to the first assumption is that in many, if not most, valuations, the valuer is required to assume that the hereditament is vacant and to let. Indeed, the concept of valuation vacant and to let was regarded by the Lands Tribunal in *Fir Mill Ltd v Royton UDC* (1960) 7 RRC 171 as one of the two key valuation assumptions (the other being the restriction of the envisaged use of the property: see below).

The purpose of the vacant and to let assumption is linked to the first statutory assumption in this way. The first assumption requires the hypothetical tenancy to begin on the AVD. The purpose of rating valuation, at its most fundamental level, is to quantify the value to the occupier of his occupation[11] of the hereditament: see for instance *Telereal Trillium* at para 33. Furthermore, under the 1988 Act, non-domestic rating is a daily tax: ss. 43(1)(a) and 45(1)(a) of the 1988 Act. In order for the value of the occupation of the property to the occupier to be fully expressed from day one of the hypothetical tenancy, it is necessary for the valuer to assume that the property is fully available to the hypothetical tenant for occupation from the tenancy's commencement. Otherwise, the hypothetical tenant would need to spend the first weeks or months of the hypothetical term securing vacant possession of the hereditament, and during that period, the hypothetical tenant would not be able to realise the fullness of the occupational value of the property.

It is important to recall, however, that the vacant and to let assumption is not itself a part of the statutory hypothesis. It is the servant of the hypothesis, not its master, and the property is assumed vacant and to let only if that assumption would further the purpose of the statutory hypothesis. There are some valuation contexts, most notably in the use of the receipts and expenditure valuation, where the vacant and to let assumption undermines the purpose of the hypothesis; where that is the

11 Or in the case of an empty property, the value to the owner of the occupation which the owner is able to commence.

case, the vacant and to let assumption is not to be adopted. This will be explored later, when we look at the R&E method.

The repairing assumption

The second assumption requires the valuer to assume that the hereditament is in a state of reasonable repair at the commencement of the tenancy, unless a reasonable landlord would consider the cost of such repairs to be uneconomic.

On one level, that is a relatively straightforward provision, the effect of which is readily understandable to any lawyer who is versed in the law of landlord and tenant and the approach taken to dilapidations.

The second assumption, however, has generated, and continues to generate, a significant amount of litigation. Indeed, over the last decade it has been one of the most controversial provisions in the whole of the 1988 Act.

The controversy relates to the relationship between a property which is in disrepair, on the one hand, and a property which has been rendered incapable of beneficial occupation because of a deliberate scheme of works, on the other. At what point does a deliberate scheme of works result in something other than a state of disrepair to be disregarded under the repairing assumption?

The full history of the repairing assumption, and of its associated controversies, is beyond the scope of this book. For present purposes, the leading authority on this issue is *Newbigin (VO) v Monk* [2017] 1 WLR 851. That case concerned a former office building which was undergoing a comprehensive scheme of redevelopment. On the material day, the contractors had removed the air conditioning, sanitary fittings, and majority of the ceiling tiles and grid, as well as about half of the raised floor. The electrical wiring had also been stripped out, and the block walls of the former WCs had been demolished. Some work had begun to instal the new WCs in their revised locations.

The VO contended, and the Court of Appeal agreed, that the property should be valued as though it were an office in a state of disrepair, despite the fact that it was in reality unusable as such.

The Supreme Court allowed the ratepayer's appeal and confirmed a nominal £1 RV for the property.[12] The Court acknowledged that the "reality principle", i.e. the principle that a hereditament should be valued as it in fact existed in reality on the material day, was an established and fundamental principle of rating law. The repairing assumption did not, and was not intended to, displace it to the extent contended for by the VO. In particular, the repairing assumption did not address "*the question of whether the premises were capable of beneficial occupation, which, in the context of a building undergoing redevelopment, is a logically prior question*" (para 20). The Court recognised an established distinction between disrepair, on the one hand, and works of "renewal, refurbishment or improvement" on the other, and held that the repairing assumption was not intended to alter that distinction (para 21).

As to the correct approach, Lord Hodge JSC endorsed the three-part test promulgated by the RSA and BPF as interveners to the appeal (para 22):

> *"where works were being carried out on an existing building, the correct approach was to proceed in this order: (i) to determine whether a property is capable of rateable occupation at all and thus whether it is a hereditament, (ii) if the property is a hereditament, to determine the mode or category of*

---

[12] The Court recognised that strictly speaking the property was not a hereditament at all, and so should have been deleted from the list, but endorsed a nominal RV as an alternative on the basis that it was a useful practice (paras 22 and 31). The VO has since abandoned that approach, and buildings which are undergoing *Monk* schemes are now deleted from the rating list altogether.

> *occupation and then (iii) to consider whether the property is in a state of reasonable repair for use consistent with that mode or category. The first two stages of that process involve the application of the reality principle. At the third stage the valuation officer applies the statutory assumption in paragraph 2(1)(b) if the reality is otherwise. In my view, this is a helpful approach where a building is undergoing redevelopment."*

The Court went on to note that, in identifying whether or not a property was in a state of disrepair or was undergoing a relevant scheme of works, the correct test is an objective one, and one which can have regard to the programme of works which is in fact being undertaken on the material day (para 23). The logic of the position was explained in this way:

> *"The premises were incapable of beneficial occupation, because, as an objective fact, they were in the process of redevelopment and no part of them was capable of beneficial use. If the works are objectively assessed as involving such redevelopment, there is no basis for applying the assumption in paragraph 2(1)(b) to override the reality principle and to create a hypothetical tenancy of the previously existing premises in a reasonable state of repair. This is both because a building under redevelopment, like a building under construction, is incapable of beneficial occupation and, in any event, the hypothetical landlord of a building undergoing redevelopment would normally not consider it economic to restore it to its prior use."*

The Court thus saw a clear relationship between the existence of a qualifying scheme of works, on the one hand, and an incapability of beneficial occupation, on the other. Given the Court's earlier comments about the correct test, that is unsurprising.

Following *Monk*, the VOA adopted a corporate approach to the Supreme Court's decision which involved an argument that the *Monk* tests were applicable if, and only if, a building was "undergoing reconstruction"; if the building was not first judged to be undergoing reconstruction, then the repairing assumption applied to deem the property in a reasonable state of repair even if it was in reality incapable of beneficial occupation on the material day.

That approach was robustly rejected by the Upper Tribunal in the second key case on the repairing assumption: *Jackson (VO) v Canary Wharf Ltd* [2019] RA 411. The Tribunal held that the VO's approach was "*plainly contrary*" to *Monk* (para 34), and that the VO's "building undergoing reconstruction" exception approach was a mistake (para 35).

The Tribunal went on to recognise, as a general principle, that (para 36):

> *"If premises are not capable of beneficial occupation they are not a hereditament. The only basis on which they may then be included in the rating list is under the convention that allows property temporarily incapable of occupation to remain in the list at a nominal value as a matter of administrative convenience, rather than deleting the entry and creating a new entry when the property once again becomes capable of beneficial occupation.*
>
> *37. The VO's acceptance in this case that the appeal property is not capable of beneficial occupation is therefore the beginning and end of the appeal."*

The Tribunal went on to explain that, in assessing whether or not a building is objectively under redevelopment, there is no need for there to be detailed programme of works; such a programme is admissible evidence, but not a requirement of the identification of a relevant scheme. Established market practice as to the approach to buildings, and indeed the established practice of the actual landlord, were also relevant considerations.

In the author's view, the Tribunal was correct that a building which is incapable of beneficial occupation is not a hereditament. It must be recalled that a hereditament is defined as property which is or may become liable to a rate, and as explained earlier, liability to a rate arises in respect of occupation (or on ownership of property which is not but could become occupied). If a property is incapable of beneficial occupation, then it is incapable of being occupied for rating purposes,[13] and if a property is incapable of being occupied, then it is not a property which can ever give rise to rating liability. And if a property can never give rise a rate, then it does not meet the s. 115 definition.

In essence, therefore, the author's view is that where a property is incapable of beneficial occupation, it is not a hereditament, and the repairing assumption (which is a valuation assumption which presupposes the existence of a hereditament: see the actual wording of para 2(1)(b)) has no role to play.

Where the repairing assumption does have a role to play is for properties which are capable of beneficial occupation, but which are in a state of some disrepair. In such scenarios, the repairing assumption assumes that disrepair to have been corrected, unless it would be uneconomic to do so. Whether works of repair are uneconomic is a question of fact based on all of the circumstances, and involves, essentially, a judgment about whether, in the circumstances, the reasonable landlord would carry out the works, or decide not to do so and let the property at a lower rent instead (*Monk* para 16, applying *Saunders v Maltby* [1976] RA 109).

13 Beneficial occupation is one of the four "ingredients" of occupation for rating purposes, the others being actual occupation (in the sense of some actual physical use of the property), exclusive occupation, and non-transient occupation. These are known as the *J S Laing* criteria, after the Court of Appeal authority which first set them out. They have since been confirmed at the highest level: see for instance the judgment of Lord Carnwath JSC in *Cardtronics UK Ltd v Sykes (VO)* [2020] 1 WLR 2184.

Tenant's covenants

The third assumption imposes, in effect, a series of covenants on the hypothetical tenant, by which the hypothetical tenant is required to bear most of the costs associated with occupying the property. Those include all rates and taxes (including non-domestic rates), insurance, and the cost of repair.

This is probably the least controversial of the assumptions. It is relevant mainly to the determination of the adjustments which need to be made to market evidence when carrying out a rental valuation (see below). In certain struggling town centres, for example, it is not uncommon for landlords to let properties on terms highly favourable to the tenant,[14] under which the landlord agrees to reimburse the tenant for its non-domestic rating liability. Where a lease is structured in such a way, the effect of the reimbursement provision needs to be adjusted out so that the rent mirrors the rating hypothesis and can be used as evidence of value.

---

14 The alternative to such favourable terms is that the landlord cannot let the property at all in these cases, and that is even les desirable for most landlords, given that they are required to pay the full empty rate on the property while it stands vacant.

CHAPTER FOUR

THE RELEVANT DATES

We now turn to consider the dates on which various factors fall to be assessed for the purposes of rating valuation.

As already explained, there are two relevant dates for valuation purposes.

The first is the **AVD**. The AVD is easy to determine – it is (or at least has always been for every rating list since 1990) the date two years before the compilation date of the list in question.

The AVD is the relevant date for assessing any factor which is not specifically prescribed by Sch 6 as a factor to be considered at the material day. In general, therefore, the AVD is the date at which matters such as supply and demand, general market conditions and economic outlook, and the legal and political landscape fall to be assessed.

The **material day** is, in broad terms, the date at which the physical and use conditions for the hereditament itself, and of its locality, fall to be assessed. The full list of factors which are to be taken as they are at the material day is set out in para 2(7) of Sch 6:

> *(a) matters affecting the physical state of the hereditament,*
>
> *(aa) matters affecting the physical enjoyment of the hereditament,*
>
> *(b) the mode or category of occupation of the hereditament,*
>
> *(c) the quantity of minerals or other substances in or extracted from the hereditament,*

> *(cc) the quantity of refuse or waste material which is brought onto and permanently deposited on the hereditament,*
>
> *(d) matters affecting the physical state of the locality in which the hereditament is situated,*
>
> *(da) matters which, though not affecting the physical state of the locality in which the hereditament is situated, are nonetheless physically manifest there, and*
>
> *(e) the use or occupation of other premises situated in the locality of the hereditament.*

The determination of the material day depends on whether the valuation is for the compilation of a list, or the alteration of a list.

When a rating list is first compiled, the material day for the whole of the list is the compilation date: para 2(5) of Sch 6. Thus, when the current (2023) list was compiled, the material day was 1 April 2023. The valuer was required, therefore, to take the para 2(7) factors as they existed on 1 April 2023, and consider how much the hereditament would have let for, on the statutory terms, if it had been offered to the market in that condition on 1 April 2021, with all of the supply and demand and wider economic considerations which were applicable on that earlier date. If the reader had not already detected it, it will now be readily apparent that a degree of imagination is required to be a rating practitioner!

The Non-Domestic Rating Act 2023 has introduced a complicating factor, in the form of para 2(ZA) to Sch 6. For the 2026 List and onwards, that provision requires the valuer to disregard any changes in the factors listed in para 2(7)(aa), (da) and (e) which occur after the AVD, to the extent that the changes are directly or indirectly attributable to any legislation, legislative provision, advice or guidance or the UK or of any other country or territory, or of anything done by any person with a view to compliance with any such legislation etc. This rather complicated provision gives general effect to legislative changes which were introduced specifically to address the COVID-19 pandemic, and give effect to the Government's intention to ensure that the general legislative and public policy landscape is an AVD rather than a material day factor.

Para 2(ZA) also affects the circumstances in which changes in those factors can warrant an alteration to a rating list after it is compiled.

When a rating list is altered after it has been compiled, either because the list was compiled inaccurately or it has become inaccurate because of a change in circumstances, the material day is determined in accordance with the Non-Domestic Rating (Material Day for List Alterations) Regulations 1992, as amended. The main provision of those regulations is reg 3. That complex provision operates as follows:

a. Where the list was inaccurate at the point of compilation, and that error is being corrected, the material day is the compilation date.

b. Where a hereditament is added to or removed from the list, including where the addition or deletion occurs because of a split or merger, or a change in a property's status as either domestic or exempt, then the material day is the date on which the circumstances giving rise to the alteration occurred.

c. Where the alteration is to give effect to a completion notice, the material day is the completion date.

d. Where the list is inaccurate because a previous alteration contained an error, the material day for the correction is the same as the material day for the initial (inaccurate) alteration.

e. In any other case, the material day depends on the mechanism by which the alteration arises. If it is caused by a proposal, then the material day is the date on which the "check" stage of the proposal process was confirmed by the proposer. This raises an important tactical matter for those advising ratepayers: where a ratepayer wishes to make a change to the list to reflect a temporary change of circumstances, the check must occur while the temporary change subsists. The check cannot be left until after the temporary change has concluded. If the alteration is not caused by a proposal, the material day is the date on which the circumstances giving rise to the alteration occurred; if that date cannot reasonably be ascertained, the material day is the date on which the VO alters the list.

As if that wasn't complicated enough, the introduction of the CCA procedure raises an added difficulty: proposers are now required to specify, in their proposals, the date on which they consider that the list ought to be altered as a result of the circumstances raised in the proposal (reg 6(4)(d) of the 2009 Regulations). The Valuation Tribunal for England has interpreted that provision as fixing the material day, in cases where a hereditament is to be added or deleted, as being the date specified in the proposal: see for instance *Aviva Investors v Bunyan (VO)* [2023] RA 11. The VTE's approach in this regard is in the author's view somewhat problematic, since it appears to limit the operation of the material day regulations by a side wind; the correctness of the VTE's approach is yet to be tested in the Upper Tribunal.

CHAPTER FIVE

THE CIRCUMSTANCES OF THE PROPERTY AND ITS LOCALITY

Finally, we turn to the circumstances which are applicable to the valuation exercise on the relevant date. The main consideration for lawyers under this heading is whether or not a factor falls within the ambit of para 2(7) of Sch 6 to the 1988 Act (which were set out in the previous chapter), since that affects the relevant date at which the factor is to be considered: if a factor is within the ambit of para 2(7) it is fixed on the material day; if it is not, it is fixed at the AVD.

The factors contained in para 2(7) are a statutory encapsulation of what is known as the "**reality principle**".[15] The reality principle initially developed through judicial decisions. It is concerned to ensure that, while the tenancy is hypothetical, the property itself is as it exists in reality. Its importance was emphasised by the Supreme Court in *Monk*, where it was described as remaining "*a fundamental principle of rating*" (para 14).

The risks of departing from reality as to the property itself have long been recognised: in *Great Western and Metropolitan Railway Cos v Kensington and Hammersmith Assessment Committees* [1916] 1 AC 23, Lord Parmoor observed, with just a hint of despair, that "*there is difficulty in the doctrine*

[15] In older cases, the reality principle is referred to as valuation *rebus sic stantibus*. The Tribunal has since sought to move away from the use of the Latin, but many valuers will still use "*rebus*" as a shorthand term for the reality principle.

of a hypothetical tenant, but if to this is added the doctrine of a hypothetical hereditament, the confusion would become hopeless" (54).

In broad terms, the reality principle as it developed in the case law was concerned with (a) physical characteristics, and (b) use characteristics, as applied to (a) the hereditament itself, and (b) the locality in which the hereditament is situated. The list of factors in para 2(7) sets out the various ways in which those points can intersect.

A full treatment of the material day factors is beyond the scope of a book on valuation. We will therefore consider only the key points applicable for each of the factors.

The physical state of the property

This is perhaps the easiest of the material day factors to understand. The hypothetical parties are, broadly speaking, required to take the physical fabric of the property as they find it, and the hypothetical tenant's bid cannot be made on the basis of development value.

There are three exceptions to the general rule that the physical state of the property is fixed at the material day:

a. Where the repairing assumption is engaged, the valuer must assume that the physical state of the property differs from reality to the extent that any disrepair which is capable of being economically corrected is assumed to have been corrected;

b. Any aspect of the property which is classified as plant and machinery is treated as present only if it is rateable under the Valuation for Rating (Plant and Machinery) (England) Regulations 2000, as amended. Any non-rateable plant and machinery (which includes items present at the property mainly in support of the occupier's trade processes, such as specialist air handling equipment: *Iceland Foods Ltd v Berry (VO)* [2018] 1 WLR 1277) is to be disregarded for valuation purposes.

c. The hypothetical tenant is able to envisage making minor alterations to the physical fabric of the hereditament. The purpose of the minor alterations rule was explained by the Court of Appeal in *Williams (VO) v Scottish and Newcastle Retail Ltd* [2001] RA 41 per Robert Walker LJ at para 74: "*The absurdity of any other view appears vividly from the circumstances of these appeals, with numerous very well-known retail chains seeking to establish their identities and brand loyalties by distinctive fascias and fittings installed in uniform, featureless units. The [physical state factor] cannot be applied so rigidly as to prevent (for instance) Burger King being considered as a possible bidder in competition with McDonald's*".

<u>The physical enjoyment of the property</u>

This is a material day factor which has received surprisingly limited judicial attention. Its purpose is to bring within the reality principle legislative or regulatory controls on how a property can be used, which are such as to bind any occupier of the property, and thus to bind the hypothetical tenant. A classic example of such a matter was the introduction of the smoking ban in July 2007: that was a matter which had a particular impact on the way in which certain kinds of premises (pubs for instance) could be physically enjoyed. Since the matter emanated from statute, rather than from the particular arrangements made by the actual landlord and the actual tenant, it formed part of the reality principle because the hypothetical tenant would be affected by it just as would any other occupier of a pub. Another matter which affects the physical enjoyment of a property for these purposes is the property's planning status: the impact of any onerous planning conditions, for instance, must be reflected in the valuation.

This limb of Sch 6 is, in many ways, a statutory manifestation of a principle enunciated by the House of Lords in *Dawkins v Ash.* The principle in question was expressed by Lord Pearce at 382; the statement is sufficiently important to the subject that it is worth setting out at length:

> *"one only excludes [from the valuer's assessment] the human realities to a limited and necessary extent, since it is only the human realities that give any value at all to hereditaments. They are excluded in so far as they are accidental to the letting of a hereditament. They are acknowledged in so far as they are essential to the hereditament itself. It is, for instance, essential to the hereditament itself that it is close to the sea and that humans will pay more highly for a house close to the sea. One can therefore take that into account in the hypothetical letting. It is, however, accidental to the house that its owner was shrewd or that the rich man happened to want it and that therefore the rent being paid is extremely high. In the same way I think it would be accidental to the hereditament that its owner intended to pull it down in the near future. For the hereditament might have had a different owner who would not pull it down. So the actual owner's intentions are thus immaterial since it is the hypothetical owner who is being considered. But when a demolition order is made by a Superior power on a hereditament within its jurisdiction different considerations apply. The order becomes an essential characteristic of the hereditament, regardless of who may be its owner or what its owner might intend."*

The distinction between matters essential to the hereditament, on the one hand, and matters accidental to the real-world letting, on the other, is a helpful way of understanding the boundaries of the reality principle in all its manifestations.

Mode or category of occupation

This limb of the reality principle serves to prevent the hypothetical tenant from realising any development value inherent in a property by changing its use.

The leading authority on this factor is *Scottish and Newcastle*. That case concerned two pubs in a shopping centre in Milton Keynes. The pubs had the same basic construction as the retail units in the shopping centre, but commanded much lower rents (less than 25% of the retail rental value). The Court of Appeal held that, in valuing the properties for rating purposes, the units' more lucrative potential as shops had to be left out of account: they were to be valued in the use that they were actually put at the material day.

The **mode or category of occupation** is to be understood by reference to the broad purpose of its use, and not applied too specifically. The Court in *Scottish and Newcastle* endorsed (para 70) as "*on the right lines*" the formulation of the Lands Tribunal in the earlier case[16] that one is to value "*a shop as a shop, but not as any particular kind of shop; a factory as a factory, but not any particular kind of factory*". Robert Walker LJ also explained the limits of the principle (para 71):

> *"It may be useful to note some situations in which the second limb of the rule, understood in this way, does not assist a ratepayer in obtaining a lower valuation. It does not assist a ratepayer who leaves half of his business premises empty, or otherwise runs his business in an half-hearted or inefficient manner; that does not go to the category of the business occupation, but to the way the particular business is run. Nor does it cast any doubt whatsoever on the decision in Robinson Brothers (Brewers) [1937] 2 KB 445, that a brewer interested in acquiring a tied house should be regarded as in the market*

16 *Fir Mill Ltd v Royton UDC* (1960) 7 RRC 171.

> *for an hypothetical tenancy of a free house; again, that goes not to the category of business for which the premises are occupied, but to the way the business is run."*

In *Hughes v Exeter CC* [2020] RA 129, the Upper Tribunal warned against the introduction of excessive sub-divisions of modes or categories of occupation by reference to specialist uses; the Tribunal's preference was for "*a broader, single mode or category containing a range of properties rather than claiming that there are narrower categories which are self-contained*" (para 205).

That broad approach has been consistently applied by the Tribunal in recent years: thus the relegation of a football club from the Premier League, via the Championship, to League One, did not involve a change in the property's mode or category of occupation despite the substantial effect of the relegation on the club's broadcasting and attendance revenues (*Wigan Football Club Ltd v Cox (VO)* [2019] UKUT 389 (LC)). Similarly, a power station had to be valued without regard to the fact that, on the material day, it had been subject to long-term mothballing and was physically incapable of generating electricity (*SSE Plc v Moore (VO)* [2023] RA 245).

Minerals and waste

The purpose of this limb is to bring within the reality principle certain aspects of the physical state of a property which undergo regular change of their very nature. In the case of a working mine, for instance, the physical state of the property, in the sense of the minerals contained in or under the land, changes on an almost daily basis, as minerals are won. Similarly, where an industrial or energy sector hereditament includes a spoil heap, that heap can grow daily as new spoil is deposited on to it.

Paras 2(7)(c) and (cc) are intended to ensure that these specialist aspects of the state of a property are reflected in the hypothesis.

In the case of minerals, the reality principle requires consideration not just of the quantity of mineral remaining in the hereditament (often referred to as the "minerals reserve"). But also the quantity already extracted from the site. The combination of knowledge of the quantity already extracted, and the time over which the extraction occurs, enables the valuer to determine the historic extraction rate. The valuer can rely on that rate as evidence of the likely future extraction rate, which is in turn relevant to the hereditament's value (*Cemex UK Operations ltd v O'Dwyer (VO)* [2019] RA 267 at para 49)

Given that these material day factors can in many cases change on a daily or weekly basis for a hereditament, the result should, on a strict reading of the statute, be a daily or weekly revaluation to reflect the material change in circumstances. In practice, the VOA has for decades adopted the approach of annual revaluations for such sites; this is generally recognised as a suitable way of reflecting the changing nature of the hereditaments in a proportionate fashion.

The physical state of the locality

Just as the physical state (in the sense identified above) of the property itself is fixed at the material day, so too is the physical state of the locality. In many cases the physical state of the locality can be just as value-significant as the state of the property itself – if the hereditament is a 5th floor office, for instance, then the state of the ground floor reception area and the staircases to the 5th floor, which form part of the locality, will be of obvious relevance.

What, though, is meant by "locality" in this context? The extent of a hereditament's locality is a fact-sensitive matter which takes into account all the circumstances, including the nature of the property and its mode or category of occupation, as well as the wider economic and technological landscape. If the hereditament is a small local corner shop, for instance, the locality may be limited to the residential streets surrounding it; if however the hereditament is a larger shop in a town centre, the locality may extend several miles to an out-of-town retail park which provides the main source of competition. For a large logistics warehouse, the locality may extend to the strategic road network for many miles around the site.

The fact-sensitive nature of the locality was recently confirmed by the VTE in *Barclays Bank Plc v Moore (VO)* (CHG100884839; 5 June 2024), in which the VTE rejected a contention form the VO that the locality of a retail unit was limited to those parts of the area within a reasonable walking distance of the hereditament.

Matters physically manifest in the locality

This is the hardest of the material day factors to understand.

It is targeted at things which are physically discernible in the locality of a property, but without actually forming a physical part of the locality itself. The quantity of traffic on a road, for instance, is something which is physically manifest in an area without actually being part of its physical fabric (the road is the same whether there are any cars on it or not).

The leading modern authority on this aspect of the reality principle is *Merlin Entertainments Ltd v Cox (VO)* [2019] RA 101, a complex and lengthy decision concerning the ramifications of a tragic crash on a rollercoaster at Alton Towers theme park, which had resulted in a number of life changing injuries.

As to the nature of this limb, the Tribunal said (para 56):

> *"it is "the matter" itself which must be "physically manifest" in the locality. It does not suffice that the matter affects the locality. We therefore see no significance in the appellant's submission that the second limb begins with the word "matters" rather than "physical matters". That opening word applies to both limbs of sub-para. (d), but under the second limb, only matters which*

> *themselves are physically present can qualify. Even then, their presence must be manifest. Here, the first definition of "manifest" in the Oxford English Dictionary is pertinent: – "Clearly revealed to the eye, mind, or judgment; open to view or comprehension; obvious"*
>
> *57. Examples of matters falling within the second limb of para. 2(7), include noise, fumes or vibration and facilities such as public transport services."*

The Upper Tribunal undertook an extensive assessment of the legislation and jurisprudential history of this limb of the reality principle, before concluding that economic or intangible matters which have caused a physical change in the locality are not themselves factors to be taken at the material day (para 146). The physical change itself is a material day factor; but the cause is not, and indeed is irrelevant to the valuation exercise.

A working example may assist. The Tribunal in *Merlin* provided one at para 156:

> *"Changes in footfall can reflect different types of change. Footfall may decrease or increase because, for example, a railway line serving the town is built or closed down or because the train services on that line are increased or reduced. Likewise, footfall may alter because of changes in bus services or because a highway or pedestrian route is created or stopped-up, or is made more or less attractive to traffic. Changes of this kind may not involve a significant change in the physical structure or state of the locality. But they are nonetheless matters which themselves are physically manifest in a town centre as something which determines one of its intrinsic qualities, namely its accessibility. Such a change would generally fall within para. 2(7)(d) and would therefore fall to be taken into account as at the date when the list is compiled, or on the material day if the relevant event occurred subsequently. It is the change in transport services or accessibility*

> *which constitutes the matter falling within para. 2(7)(d) and which may therefore amount to a material change in circumstances calling for a revaluation."*

The Tribunal emphasised that in such cases, the change in footfall *per se* is not the para 2(da) factor, because it may be caused by something which has nothing to do with the physical characteristics of the locality (such as a change in the national, regional or local unemployment rate) (para 158).

In the Tribunal's example, the material day factor is the change in the bus timetable; the change in footfall rate is not itself a change in a material day factor, but is <u>evidence</u> of the physical manifestation of the change in the bus timetable. The reason <u>why</u> the bus timetable has changed is likely to be an intangible or economic consideration (it may be the result of a local authority initiative to encourage spending in town centre shops to counter an economic slowdown, for instance) is not a material day factor, because such economic causative factors are taken as they are at the AVD.

Lawyers can be of considerable assistance to valuers in helping them to distinguish between, cause, manifestation, and evidence in this context.

<u>Use and occupation of premises in the locality</u>

This is a reflection of the use limb of the reality principle into the area beyond the hereditament itself.

If a shop at one end of a road changes its use to a pub, that will clearly have implications for an existing pub at the other end of the road, through the introduction of competition. Para 2(7)(e) is designed to bring such alterations within the scope of the reality principle, and thus to be a matter to be taken as it in fact stood at the material day.

This aspect of the reality principle is drafted in different language to the corresponding provision which concerns the use of the hereditament itself. Para 2(7)(b) of Sch 6 concerns changes to the "mode or category of occupation" of the hereditament, and as already explained, that is a broad concept: changes of use within the mode or category (the change of use of a shop from a butcher to a cheesemonger, for instance), would not be relevant alterations under para 2(7)(b).

By contrast, para 2(7)(e) concerns the "use and occupation" of other premises. There are two implications of the difference in language.

The first is that a change in the use of premises can be a material day factor even if the mode or category of occupation has not changed. The hereditament itself must be treated as a "shop, but no particular kind of a shop", whereas shops in the locality can and should be treated as a shoe shop, a grocery etc.

The second implication is that a change in whether or not a property is occupied at all can be taken into account. There are many instances in which a change in the occupational status of other properties in the vicinity of a hereditament may affect its value. The classic example of such a change is the closure of the anchor store in a shopping mall: the effect of that closure is almost inevitably to reduce the footfall to the shopping centre overall, which has ramifications for the trade potential of all of the other units in the mall.

PART TWO

VALUATION

CHAPTER SIX

VALUATION METHODOLOGIES AND THEIR SELECTION

Having applied the principles in Part 1 and established the question for the valuer, the next matter for consideration is how valuers go about answering the valuation question.

It is important to stress, at the outset of Part 2, that the selection and operation of valuation methodologies is not a matter of law. That was confirmed by the Upper Tribunal in the important case of *Hughes (VO) v York Museums and Gallery Trust* [2017] RA 302, a case to which we will return several times. The Tribunal observed (para 112) that:

> *"Ascertainment of the rent at which premises might reasonably be expected to let on the statutory assumptions is a question of fact, not one of law. The selection of the most appropriate technique to be employed in answering that question is a matter of valuation judgment rather than legal precedent."*

While the law does not dictate the answer to a valuation question, it is nevertheless the case that the Courts and Tribunals have established a number of principles of valuation, which inform the way in which the valuer goes about the task of valuing a property in accordance with the rating hypothesis.

Valuers – in the VOA, in private practice, and via their membership of the Lands Chamber of the Upper Tribunal (and the Lands Tribunal before it) – have developed a number of approaches which are available to value properties for rating purposes.

The main methods will be examined in the following chapters of this Part. Before turning to those methods, however, it is worth exploring the principles and guidance on the choice of valuation method.

The starting point is the decision of the Court of Appeal in *Garton v Hunter (VO) (No 1)* [1969] 2 QB 37. That case concerned a caravan site. The ratepayer's valuer valued the hereditament using the contractor's basis, and the VO relied on the R&E method. The Lands Tribunal ruled that neither of those valuation methods was admissible as evidence, because there existed rental evidence from the subject property itself.

On appeal to the Court of Appeal, Lord Denning MR stressed that any valuation method was admissible as a matter of law. The valuer is not required to choose any particular method, nor is the tribunal required to decide the best method and disregard all others. The goodness or badness of the evidence goes only to the weight to be attached to it, and not to its admissibility (44).

Lord Denning MR concluded (45) that:

> *"the tribunal was wrong in limiting the inquiry to the actual rent and making adjustments to it. It should also have taken into account the estimates given by the opposing valuers on the "contractor's basis" and the "profits basis". From the sum of all the available material it should have come to an estimate of the sum which a hypothetical tenant would pay as rent for this caravan site."*

The result is that the valuer is not required to adopt any one method. Indeed, in difficult cases where no one method is reliable on its own, there may be considerable merit in the valuer adopting multiple methods of valuation, and considering all of them as a "basket of evidence" in reaching his overall judgment as to the value of the property.

There are many instances of properties being valued in accordance with more than one method. The valuer might adopt the R&E method as the primary valuation method, for instance, but sense check the result using the shortened method; the valuer might value the land and buildings of a property using the rentals method, but the plant and machinery element using the contractor's basis; or the valuer might value the landlord-provided elements of an office building using the comparables method but value the tenant's fit out elements using an amortised cost basis. There is no rule of law, nor any rule of valuation, which dictates the approach in any given case: the valuer's task is to find the method or combination of methods which best answers the question posed by the statutory hypothesis.

The author suggests that, in the selection of the method or methods to be adopted, the valuer could helpfully bear in mind the following points of principle:

a. As the following chapters will show, each and every method has its strengths and weaknesses. The particular circumstances of a property may render a given method unsuitable in some particular respect, and such unsuitability must be borne in mind in deciding the weight (if any) to apply to any given approach. The contractor's basis, for example, is notoriously unreliable in cases where the fabric of the existing building is itself of cultural or historical value.

b. It is critical that the valuer explain the reasoning which underlies the choice of methods which is made. The rationale for the choice of the primary method, and any secondary methods, should be set out as a part of the valuer's expert evidence. Similarly, if a method is rejected as of no use, it can be helpful to explain why it has been rejected. This latter point is particularly important where another valuer is using the rejected method in his own valuation (even if only as a sense check).

c. Where there is a methodological dispute between valuers, it is immensely helpful for the valuer to value the property using the other valuer's methodology as well as his own. If valuer A considers that a hereditament is best valued using the R&E method, for instance, whereas valuer B considers that the contractor's basis is preferable, valuer A should value the property on both the R&E and contractor's bases, as alternatives. Otherwise, the valuer risks putting all his eggs in one basket, and if the methodological dispute is resolved in favour of the other side in an appeal, then the valuer has nothing further to contribute.

d. Of course, it may be that the valuer agrees with the other side's valuation on a given method, but simply considers that the method is unsuitable *ab initio*. In a purely methodological dispute of this kind, it is helpful for the valuers to agree a statement of common ground setting out their agreed valuations on the alternative methods.

e. In all cases, the valuer must remember that the task he is undertaking is to value the property under the statutory hypothesis. If any given method is in conflict with the hypothesis in any way, then it is the method which must be altered to accommodate the hypothesis, not vice versa. Valuers often refer to the most important stage in any valuation as the "stand back and look" stage, which is the point at which the result of the applied methodology is sense checked against the statutory hypothesis. This stage can seem more nebulous, and less scientific or arithmetical, than the earlier stages of a valuation. That does not however reduce its importance; on the contrary, the "stand back and look" stage is the most important part of any valuation. Ultimately, valuation is more of an art than a science, and a valuer who follows a given method too strictly risks missing the critical element of professional judgment.

The *Lotus* hierarchy

Any lawyer who practises in the field of rating valuation will, sooner or later, hear mention of the ***Lotus* hierarchy**. This is a concept which is useful, but which is often misunderstood and misapplied.

The approach is named for the decision of the Lands Tribunal in *Lotus and Delta Ltd v Culverwell (VO)* [1976] RA 141. In that case, a very eminent valuer Member, Mr J H Emlyn Jones FRICS, set out a series of propositions for the guidance of valuers in choosing their approach.

Those propositions were distilled and summarised by an equally eminent valuer member of the Upper Tribunal – Peter McCrea FRICS – in *Lamb (VO) v Go Outdoors Ltd* [2015] RA 475. That summary is sufficiently succinct and clearly expressed that it is worth setting out in full (para 38):

> *"(i) Where the hereditament which is the subject of consideration is actually let, that rent should be taken as a starting point.*
>
> *(ii) The more closely the circumstances under which the rent was agreed both as to time, subject matter and conditions, relate to the statutory assumptions, the more weight should be attached to it.*
>
> *(iii) Where rents of similar properties are available they too are properly to be looked at through the eye of the valuer in order to confirm or otherwise the level of value indicated by the actual rent of the subject hereditament.*
>
> *(iv) Rating assessments of other comparable properties are also relevant. When a valuation is prepared these assessments are to be taken as indicating comparative values as estimated by the valuation officer. In subsequent proceedings on that list therefore they can properly be referred to as giving some indication of that opinion.*

> *(v) In light of all the evidence an opinion can then be formed of the value of the subject hereditament, the weight to be attributed to the different types of evidence depending on the one hand on the nature of the actual rent and, on the other hand, on the degree of comparability found in other properties.*
>
> *(vi) In cases where there is no evidence of rents of comparable properties, a review of other assessments may be helpful, but in such circumstances it would clearly be more difficult to reject the evidence of the actual rent."*

There are two important points to be made about the *Lotus* hierarchy.

The first is that it is not, in truth, a hierarchy at all. Nor is it a set of rules which must be followed. Rather, as the Upper Tribunal has stressed (see for instance *Go Outdoors* at para 39), the *Lotus* propositions are guidance on the usefulness of different types of evidence, and are not to be followed slavishly. The focus must always be on the statutory hypothesis.

The second point is that the *Lotus* propositions are plainly directed at those classes of hereditament for which rents are likely to exist. The propositions are useful where, for instance, the valuer is concerned with a shop or an office. The propositions are plainly not helpful in valuing those classes of property which are seldom if ever let: the surveyor charged with valuing a nuclear power station, say, or an airport, will find little assistance from the *Lotus* propositions.

CHAPTER SEVEN

THE RENTALS METHOD

For the lawyer venturing into the world of rating valuation, the method most likely to be encountered in the early stages is the **rentals method**.

This is by far the most common of the valuation methods, and in many ways the easiest to apply. It is suitable for those classes of property which tend, in the real world, to be occupied by tenants rather than by owner-occupiers. Offices, retail outlets, warehouses, and other high street commercial units are typically valued using this approach.

The premise of the rentals method is simple: where there is real-world evidence of the letting either of the subject hereditament itself, or of properties similar to the subject hereditament (known to valuers as "**comparables**"), then those real-world rents will provide evidence of the RV of the hereditament by a process of adjustment and comparison.

The complexity of the rentals method lies in the process of "analysing" the real-world evidence.

Analysis is necessary because, in practice, almost no property is ever let in the real world on terms which precisely mirror those posited by the statutory hypothesis. Even where the hereditament itself has been let in the real world, that letting is unlikely to have taken place on the AVD itself; nor is it likely that the terms of the letting will match the terms of the hypothetical tenancy.

To the extent that rental evidence departs from the hypothesis, that departure needs to be accounted for, and adjustments made to the resultant rent, if it is to provide evidence of the value of the hereditament on the statutory terms. By way of example, under the statutory hypothesis, the hypothetical tenant's rent is due to the hypothetical landlord as soon as the hypothetical tenancy commences: the statutory hypothesis does not posit any form of rent-free period to make the property more attractive to the tenant. If, in the real world, the tenant of a comparable received the benefit of a rent-free period at the commencement of their tenancy, then the valuer's task is to calculate what the rent under that lease would have been if no rent-free period had been agreed.

Broadly speaking, there are four classes of adjustments for which analysis may be required:

1. Temporal
2. Contractual
3. Physical
4. Locational

The first two are relevant in virtually every case; the latter two are usually relevant only where rents on comparables are being analysed.

General observations on rental analysis

As we saw in the previous chapter when looking at the *Lotus* hierarchy, it is an established principle that the closer the rent is to the statutory hypothesis, the more weight it will carry. The concomitant is that the more adjustments are required to a rent, the less evidentially weighty it is likely to be in the basket of evidence.

The reason for that is clear: every time a rent is adjusted, the grounding of the evidence in the real market becomes slightly weaker, and real-world market signals are replaced by valuer judgment and skill. If only one adjustment is required, and that adjustment is slightly inaccurate, then it may not make much difference to the overall accuracy of the evidence;

where multiple adjustments are made, however, there is a greater risk of multiple small inaccuracies compounding one another and distorting the RV which the evidence eventually suggests.

That concern should not be pressed too far, however. The bare fact that multiple adjustments are required does not, of itself, weaken the resultant evidence, if the valuer can show that each of the adjustments has been undertaken on a robust and reliable basis. That was confirmed by the Upper Tribunal in *Lamb (VO) v Go Outdoors* at para 43, in the context of a "heavily incentivised" lease:

> "*[Counsel for the VO] submitted that the very fact that the lease was heavily incentivised, and that the rent required significant adjustment to arrive at a notional rent on the rating hypothesis, reduced the weight that could be placed on the adjusted rent. I agree that adjustments are required but do not accept that they render this contemporaneous evidence of a letting in the open market any less valuable. In fact, in this case although the incentives required to be devalued, there was no disagreement over how that should be done, which gives me further confidence in the evidential value of the actual letting of the appeal property. Mr Lamb agreed that the relevant RICS Guidance Note's purpose was to provide guidance on the devaluation of incentives, rather than to reject them out of hand. He also accepted that they were a general feature of the market. I am therefore satisfied that the letting is capable of providing powerful evidence of the rent at which the hereditament might reasonably be expected to let on the AVD.*"

Even where multiple adjustments are required, and even if the resultant weight is reduced, the evidence produced by the rentals method can remain very persuasive. As the Upper Tribunal explained in the *York Museums* case (para 113):

> "*The greater the adjustments required to be made to mirror the statutory valuation assumptions or other differences, the less*

> *reliable a guide the comparable may be, but valuation by the comparative method always has the advantage over other methods of being rooted in evidence of the behaviour of real landlords and tenants in the market in which it is to be assumed the subject premises are being let."*

More recently, in *Bunyan v Acenden Ltd* [2023] RA 213, the Upper Tribunal stressed the role of valuer judgment in dealing with imperfections arising from rental analysis (para 59):

> *"Sometimes the outcome [of rental analysis] is not entirely convincing, but that is inevitable when analysing quite complex transactions. It is important for consistency that the same approach is applied to the comparable evidence as to the letting of [the subject hereditament] itself. A proper response to imperfections in the analysis is not to abandon the comparative method of valuation but instead to rely on judgment rather than arithmetic, to avoid the temptation to place too much weight on a single transaction and to bear in mind the general patterns which emerge from the evidence as a whole."*

In other words: do not forget that valuation is more an art than a science.

In general, it does not matter in what order the various factors are accounted for in the analysis process: if the analysis is undertaken correctly, the same end result should occur irrespective of the sequence in which the adjustments are made.

With those general observations in mind, we turn to the four classes of adjustment.

Temporal adjustments

Temporal adjustment is required because leases are seldom if ever executed on the AVD itself. Since property markets rise and fall over time (sometimes very rapidly), it is necessary, where a rent has been agreed at a date other than the AVD, to form a judgment on whether or not the market has risen or fallen between the AVD and the date of the agreement of the rent, and to account for that rise or fall by increasing or decreasing the rent accordingly.

Where the time period in question is a matter of weeks or months, there is seldom a difficulty in agreeing the basis of the adjustment, or of making it on a robust basis. There comes a point, however, where the distance of the rent from the AVD is so significant that even an adjusted rent carries limited weight. That is because (a) the longer the period of adjustment, the more difficult it can be to capture the movement of the market in a single percentage figure, and (b) over time, the market can change not only in respect of basic prices, but also in terms of the dynamics of the market itself. It may be, for instance, that the supply-demand relationship shifts in such a way that not only do unit prices change, but the normal length of lease terms also changes, so that an added layer of complexity is added to the adjustment required.

There has been some debate in recent appeals about the date on which the real-world parties can be said to have "agreed" a rent for the purposes of adjustment: is it the date of the agreement itself, or the date on which the parties enter into heads of terms to inform the negotiations towards the lease?

In the author's view, the correct date to adopt is the date on which the parties become contractually bound by the proposed rent, i.e. the date of the lease or (if earlier) the agreement for lease. A heads of terms is not an "agreement" to anything, but is instead a springboard for discussions which may or may not result in the alteration of the heads of terms indicative rent. If, on entering a contractual agreement, the parties decide not to change the rent in the heads of terms, that is probably not because they regard themselves as having already agreed it, but because they regard the heads of terms rent as remaining appropriate in the market conditions prevailing at the time of the contract. It follows that the contractual date is the relevant date for adjustment. It remains to be seen whether the tribunals will agree with this analysis.

Contractual adjustments

This is the largest, and generally the most complex, class of required adjustment. It is concerned with the (almost inevitable) differences between the terms of the agreement entered into by the parties, and the terms of the hypothetical tenancy posited by Sch 6 to the 1988 Act.

It will be recalled that the hypothetical tenancy has a number of characteristics as defined by the 1988 Act: it is for a term of years with a reasonable prospect of continuance; the hypothetical tenant's occupation commences on the AVD; the property is in a reasonable state of repair; and the tenant bears the costs of occupation associated with the property (repairing, paying rates, insuring the property etc).

It is very rare indeed for a tenancy to be executed in the real world which has all of the statutory features, and no others. The task of the valuer, faced with such differences, is to work out what the rent would have been if the missing feature were included in the deal, or if the extra-statutory feature were excluded from it.

Where a market in a given area or at a given time is particularly weak, so that landlords struggle to secure tenants for their properties, real-world leases may include a significant number of features to incentivise the tenant to take the property. See for instance *Ballcroft Estates Ltd v Virk (VO)* [2022] RA 313, which concerned a hereditament in Kidderminster town centre, and in which the rents for analysis contained numerous features to attract tenants into the town centre following the opening of an out-of-town retail park.

The range of features which may require adjustment under this head is very broad, and the approach taken to accounting for such differences is quintessentially a matter for the judgment of the valuer rather than for legal advice. Rather than attempt to address all of the possible contractual adjustments which may arise, the general approach of valuers can be illustrated by an example: the treatment of rent-free periods.

Rent-free periods are common features of deals, particularly in the office market. Broadly speaking, rent-free periods can be provided for one of two reasons. The first, which is very common, is to account for the fact that the tenant has taken the property in an incomplete state, and requires time to finish the fitting out of the property. Since the tenant cannot beneficially occupy the property until it is fitted out, rent-free periods (three or six months is standard) are agreed between the parties to reflect the fact that, for a period of time at the very start of the lease, the tenant will not be using the property for its intended purpose, but preparing it for use for its intended purpose. The rating hypothesis assumes that the hereditament is in existence and ready for occupation on day one of the hypothetical tenancy; any such rent free period therefore needs to be adjusted out.

The second type of rent-free period is by way of a general incentive to the tenant to encourage him to enter the lease, in circumstances where the tenant is in a superior position in the market than the landlord. Again, there is no place in the rating hypothesis for such an incentive, so the valuer needs to calculate what rent the parties would have agreed, to reflect their respective strengths and weaknesses in the market, if no rent-free period had been agreed.

As rent-free periods of any kind are a benefit to the tenant, the effect of adjusting out a rent-free period will be to reduce the rent below the headline rent under the actual lease: the tenant would have agreed a lower rent if it had not received the incentive.

The way in which rent-free periods are actually accounted for is a matter for the valuer, and beyond the scope of this book. There are a number of ways to make such an adjustment, and no "right" answer (*Acenden* para 49, adopting the RICS guidance on the analysis of commercial lease transactions).

An issue which can arise is the period over which a rent-free period should be analysed. The longer the period, the higher the analysed rent, because the depressing effect of the rent-free period on the rent will be spread over a wider timeframe. In the rating context,[17] the preferred practice is to account for the rent-free period across the whole of the lease term, unless the lease contains a tenant's break clause, in which case the incentive is accounted to the break date (*Acenden* para 58). The reason for that is that, in the market, the granting of inducements such as rent-free periods is often given by landlords in exchange for the certainty of income which a lease provides, and from the viewpoint of the lease negotiations, that certainty does not persist beyond the break date. If, however, a lease contains provisions which makes the tenant's exercise of the break clause unlikely (the exercise may be accompanied by particularly onerous penalties, for instance; or the tenant may receive further inducements if it does not exercise its break clause), then that logic may not apply and analysis over a longer period may be required. Again, it must be stressed that this is not a matter of law, but a matter of valuer judgment.

Other contractual provisions which may require adjustment and analysis include:

a. The provision by the landlord of a capital contribution to the tenant (these can take the form of payments to the tenant in lieu of the landlord carrying out certain works to the property; or they can take the form of a lump-sum up-front payment from the landlord in place of a rent-free period);

---

17 A different approach has been adopted in other contexts, such as rent review valuation.

b. The payment of a premium by the tenant to the landlord;

c. A "stepped" rent, whereby the amount of rent payable for a period after the conclusion of any rent-free period is not the full headline rent, but a percentage of it;

d. Rents which are inclusive of any of the items of expenditure which the hypothesis requires the hypothetical tenant to bear, including non-domestic rates, insurance, or a service charge; and

e. A rent which reflects the value to a tenant of non-rateable items in the property (this can arise where, for instance, a tenant takes over a former tenant's lease on assignment, and the rent includes an element to reflect the fact that the former tenant has left valuable furniture or equipment in place).

Physical adjustments

Physical adjustments are required where the fabric of the comparable property differs from the subject hereditament in a way which requires the rent itself to be adjusted. Even where there is a rent on the subject property itself, that rent may not precisely match the hereditament shown in the list and which is to be valued for rating purposes: a hereditament may be let on two separate leases, for instance, or may include loading or parking spaces which form separate hereditaments.

It is rare for two properties to be of exactly the same size and layout. The way in which this is accounted for is by valuation using a "unit price" – the value of a property is expressed as a price per square metre,[18] and that

---

18 Confusingly, in some sectors and for some purposes the market prefers to express the unit price per square foot – in such cases, it is good practice for the lawyer to encourage the valuer to use a consistent unit in his own expert's reports and analyses, to avoid confusion.

unit price can then be applied to any given property of a relevant type to obtain the RV by multiplying the unit price by the size of the building.[19]

In the context of retail units, an adjusted form of the unit price approach calling "zoning" can be adopted. Zoning recognises that, in a shop, the space nearest to the window is the most valuable space. The unit price therefore varies depending on how near the space is to the window, with the band nearest the window (known as "zone A") being valued at the full unit price, the next band back ("zone B") at half the zone A unit price, zone C at half the zone B unit price, and so on. Zones run the full width of the shop's frontage, and by convention are 20 feet deep. Where the zoning approach is adopted, it is common to express the size of the hereditament "in terms of zone A" (or "ITZA"), in which the area of the shop is converted to give the size which would apply if the whole unit were zone A. By way of example, if a retail unit is 100 square metres, of which 40 square metres is zone A, 40 square metres is zone B and 20 square metres is zone C, its size ITZA will be 65 square metres (the whole of the zone A space, half of the zone B space, and a quarter of the zone C space). Expressing size ITZA is arithmetically convenient, as the unit price can be applied to the ITZA area without modification.

The use of the unit price concept eliminates much of the need for physical adjustment between properties.

---

[19] There are a range of ways in which size can be expressed for buildings. Shops and offices, for instance, are measured by reference to their "net internal area", which captures the useable space within a building and excludes things like staircases and the thickness of structural walls. By contrast, warehouses are measured using "gross internal area", which includes all of the space within a building but leaves out of account the thickness of the external walls. "Gross external area", which includes the thickness of the external walls, is not used for rating purposes, but can arise when valuing houses for Council Tax purposes, for example.

There are, however, a number of physical differences between a subject property and the comparables which may require a further adjustment to the unit price.

A commonly encountered adjustment in the office context is the quantum allowance. The basic principle is that the larger the amount of space included in a lease, the less occupational flexibility the tenant has and the less likely the tenant is to need all of the space. The result is that, in many instances, as the size of the space contained in a lease goes up, the unit price goes down. If a comparable is considerably larger or smaller than the subject hereditament, and if market signals indicate that quantum considerations are engaged, the unit price indicated by the analysis of the comparable's rent may need to be adjusted to reflect the quantum effect.

At the time of writing, by far the most controversial physical adjustment relates to what is known as "category B", or tenant's, fit out works.

The nature of the issue was explained in the *Acenden* appeal at para 1:

> *"Modern high quality office buildings are usually offered to the letting market in a "Category A" condition. If the building has been newly constructed or recently refurbished, its owner will typically have installed raised floors and suspended ceilings, basic mechanical and electrical services including lighting and air-conditioning, a fire detection system and basic internal finishes. By marketing the building in this condition, the owner will hope to generate interest from the widest range of potential occupiers. Once a letting has been achieved, the new tenant will be free to fit the building out to meet its own requirements. The tenant's fitting out work will bring the building into a "Category B" condition and is likely to include the installation of kitchens and tea points, partitioning, the re-routing of air- conditioning and power points to accommodate its preferred layout, and the addition of IT infrastructure."*

The difficulty arises because, for rating purposes, it is the property in its Category B fitted condition with which the valuer is concerned: a property in Category A condition is by definition not ready for occupation for its intended purpose, and is thus not a hereditament at all: *Arbuckle Smith & Co Ltd v Greenock Corp* [1960] AC 813.[20] The operation of the market, however, means that in the large majority of cases rents are agreed for properties in Category A condition. The result is a significant disparity between the signals provided by the market, and the question which the valuer is required to answer for the purposes of rating.

During the course of the 2017 rating list, the disparity between market evidence and the hereditaments for valuation in the prime office sector became controversial. The VO's preferred approach has been to value offices in two stages: first, the Category A value is determined using the rentals method; a sum is then added on to that Category A value, known as "virtual rent", to reflect the value of the Category B elements, calculated by amortising the cost to the tenant of fitting them.[21]

This issue was addressed by the Upper Tribunal in *Acenden,* which was something of an unofficial test case. The Upper Tribunal firmly rejected the ratepayer's contention that the appeal hereditament in its Category B state was worth the same as the property in its Category A state (para 109). Equally, however, the Tribunal saw difficulties with the VO's "virtual rent" approach (para 85):

> *"Both experts approached the valuation of Ascot House in its Category B condition by adding an amount to reflect the value of the tenant's fitting-out works to the rental value derived from the letting of the building in its original Category A condition.*

---

20 Unless it has been the subject of a completion notice, a potentially complex area of rating law which is beyond the scope of this book.

21 The methodology involved in valuation by reference to construction cost is explored further below, in the chapter on the contractor's basis of valuation.

> *In principle there is nothing wrong with that approach. Faced with limited direct evidence of new comparable lettings in Category B condition it might be the only possible approach, although that is not the case here. But it gives rise to a number of issues and uncertainties. It assumes that there is a consistent relationship between the cost of fitting-out works and the enhancement of rental value over and above a Category A figure established by market evidence. But that is simply an assumption, and it is not itself confirmed or supported by market evidence. Nor, in the absence of evidence, is there agreement in principle (at least in this case) about how the capital cost of works is to be translated into an annual rental value."*

The Tribunal went on to describe the two-stage approach as "unsatisfactory", and considered that the appropriate valuation approach was to seek a high-quality basket of market evidence of both Category A and Category B lettings, so that the differential between the value of Category A and Category B space can be understood (para 109).

Despite its status as a test case for the issue, it is fair to say that the Upper Tribunal's decision has not been fully accepted by the rating community. In a subsequent pair of appeals before the VTE (*Mando Group Ltd and Shoosmiths LLP v Hitchings (VO)*), the ratepayer contended that the market signals indicated that there was no differential between Category A and Category B values for the office sectors under consideration, whereas the VO contended that the only appropriate way to value the property was using the two-stage approach, since market evidence of Category B lettings almost always arise following a business failure of some kind, whereas the hypothetical tenancy is unaffected by such considerations. The ratepayer's argument runs up against the *Acenden* "firm rejection" of an absence of a differential; and the VO's approach relies on a methodology described in *Acenden* as unsatisfactory, and rejects the approach actually used by the Tribunal in *Acenden* on the basis of the "business failure" principle (which was not argued before the Upper Tribunal). At the time of writing, the result of the VTE appeals in *Mando* and *Shoosmiths* is awaited. It seems clear, however, that *Acenden* is not going to be the final word on this subject.

Locational adjustments

The final class of adjustments concerns the location of the comparables and the subject property. As anyone with even a passing familiarity with the property market will be aware, location is one of the key drivers of property value, and that is as true for the commercial markets as it is for the residential market. A logistics warehouse located close to a motorway junction is likely to be more valuable than an otherwise identical one located further from the junction; a shop with a frontage on to a major thoroughfare in a shopping mall will be more valuable than one fronting on to a smaller side passageway; an office in the heart of a city's commercial district will be more attractive to tenants than one on the periphery of the district; and so on. Valuers are well-versed in making adjustments to account for such features as these.

Locational considerations can work vertically as well as horizontally. In some contexts it may be more or less attractive for a property to be located on an upper floor or a multi-storey building. If the market indicators suggest that this is a consideration for tenants, then the unit price may need to be adjusted if the subject property is in a more or less attractive vertical location than the relevant comparable.

The limitations of the method

Where there is good quality rental evidence which is capable of reasonably reliable adjustment, then the rentals method is suitable for use, and will generally be the preferred method. The method is less reliable where, for whatever reason, the nature of the rental evidence available is so far removed from the statutory hypothesis that it cannot be reliably analysed.

Similarly, and obviously, the method depends on the property class in question being of a kind that is occupied by tenants on something at least loosely resembling the hypothetical tenancy. There are many classes of property, however, which are almost always occupied by owners who hold the property on either a freehold or long leasehold basis. A commercial airport, a sewerage works, or a power station, for instance, will not be occupied on anything remotely resembling a tenancy year to year. In such cases, alternative valuation approaches need to be adopted.

CHAPTER EIGHT

COMPARABLE ASSESSMENTS AND THE TONE OF THE LIST

As we have seen, the rentals method involves valuing a property by reference to the rents on comparable properties.

This chapter is concerned with a similar method: valuation by reference to **comparable assessments.**

The premise of this method is similar to that of the rentals method. The difference is that, rather than using the rents of comparable properties as the source of valuation information against which to assess the subject property, the valuer uses the RVs in the rating list of those comparable properties instead.

Once the comparables are identified, the analysis process for arriving at an RV for the subject property is very similar to that of the rentals method, at least as regards to physical and locational analysis. The valuer does not, however, have to concern himself with either temporal or contractual analysis: the data point here is not rent but RV, so by definition the data point has already been adjusted to the AVD and to the terms of the statutory hypothesis.

One distinct advantage of this method of valuation is the availability of data. If a property is a non-domestic hereditament shown in a rating list, then it will have an RV associated with it. So if the valuer finds a comparable, then it is guaranteed that there will be an RV which the valuer can use in his valuation. Put another way, this approach to valuation never suffers from the problem of scarcity of data which can undermine a rentals valuation (or even render it impossible).

One of the key points to understand about valuation using comparable assessments is that, as a method, the inputs on which the valuer relies are one step removed from the market itself. Under a rentals valuation, the sources of data (i.e. the comparables' rents) come directly from the market. A real-world rent is direct evidence as to the value of the property in question, based on the real-world negotiations of real-world landlords and tenants. As we saw in the previous chapter, that 'rooting' in the real world is what gives the rentals method its evidential force. By contrast, under the comparable assessments method, the valuer is not relying on direct market signals, but is instead relying on the opinions of other valuers: ultimately, an RV is simply a valuer's opinion as to property value.

Because it is one step removed from the market, one of the central issues which a valuer must considering using this method is the weight which can be attached to the opinion of value underlying the comparable RV. The greater the degree of consideration and analysis given to a comparable hereditament's RV when it is set, the weightier it will be as evidence.

As a matter of principle, the weight which can be attached to an RV follows a hierarchy:

a. The weightiest evidence is an RV which was set by a decision of the Upper Tribunal (Lands Chamber). The valuer members of the Upper Tribunal are some of the finest rating surveyors in the country, with extensive experience and expertise, and their determinations are made following relatively formal judicial hearings in which detailed expert valuation evidence is given and tested. The RV which results from this process has thus been analysed and considered in a detailed way, and the resultant opinion of value is as robust as can arise in the rating system.

b. Next are RVs which are set by decisions of the VTE. The VTE, like the Upper Tribunal, arrives at its decisions following consideration of the evidence at a hearing; the VTE is not however as senior a body as the Upper Tribunal, and its consideration of evidence is generally less detailed and comprehensive than that of the Upper Tribunal.

c. Next are RVs which have been subject to agreement between the parties through the CCA process. While a settled RV has not received judicial consideration and determination, it may nevertheless represent a professional "meeting of minds" between two expert valuers,[22] and where two valuers agree on an RV, it will be weightier than if the RV is the work of a single valuer. Care must be taken, however, not to attribute unjustified motives or opinions to the ratepayer's valuer. A VO valuer is subject to the duty contained in s. 41 of the 1988 Act to maintain an accurate list, and is thus legally precluded from entering into an agreement on a "commercial" basis. By contrast, a rating surveyor retained as a ratepayer's agent is under no such duty. An agent's agreement may be the result of the agent's opinion and the VO's opinion on the correct RV being the same; equally, however, the agent's agreement may be because his client has instructed him to agree the RV despite the agent's professional view that the RV is too high. Such instructions may (and commonly do) occur because the client does not want to incur the expense and risk of litigation, and is willing as a matter of commercial judgment to pay the price of an excessive RV to avoid that risk and expense. Similarly, the vagaries of the transitional relief scheme[23] mean that, in some circumstances, the amount of rates paid by a

---

22 The CCA process is usually deal with on the ratepayer side by a valuer acting as agent, rather than by a legal representative.

23 Transitional relief is a mechanism designed to "smooth out" the change in the amount of rats payable by the ratepayer when one rating list ends and the next one is compiled.

ratepayer actually goes down if a higher RV is agreed. It must never be forgotten that, while valuers are professionally interested in valuation, the ratepayer itself is generally more interested in the bottom line of rates payable. As the Lands Tribunal noted as long ago as the 1970s, a ratepayer's acquiescence to a list entry "*may represent less an acceptance of value than an acceptance of rate liability*": *Lamb (VO) v Minards* [1974] RA 153. The same point is true for the component parts of an agreed valuation: as the Upper Tribunal noted in *Hobbs v Gidman* [2017] RA 123 at para 63, "*in the end, the decision to settle any outstanding proposal was made by the ratepayer client and in some instances that decision will be driven more by the effect of a settlement on the actual rates bill than any desire to necessarily agree a specific rate for an individual item of the assessment.*" If an agreement is to be given enhanced weight, therefore, the valuer needs to be satisfied that it really does represent a professional meeting of minds on value.

d. Next in the hierarchy are RVs which have been determined by the VO at the challenge stage of CCA, and not appealed. While the RV in this case is referable to the work of a single valuer – the VO – a challenge stage determination typically involves a more detailed consideration of an individual property than may have been the case when the property's RV was first entered in the list. this is particularly true for the "bulk" property classes (like offices and shops) where thousands of valuations are carried out by the VO for each new list. Valuers sometime contend that the ratepayer's failure to appeal the challenge decision adds further weight to RVs determined at the challenge stage: as already explained however, the lack of appeal may be more to do with commercial considerations than with an acceptance that the VO's challenge decision is correct.

e. At the bottom of the hierarchy are those RVs which have been subject to no further consideration since they were entered in the list. Such RVs represent an opinion of value which was formed by an employee of the VOA who will have received at least some professional training in rating valuation (though not all such valuations are done by a fully qualified rating surveyor), and to that extent they carry at least some evidential value. It is sometimes contended that an RV which has been unchallenged for a prolonged period is weightier than one which has not been in the list for very long. There is a degree of truth to that (particularly when it comes to establishing a tone of the list – see below), but again, the absence of challenge does not necessarily equate to an agreement as to accuracy. Similarly, a ratepayer's ability to commence the CCA process for a hereditament exists until the next list is compiled[24], and a lack of challenge may be because a ratepayer is waiting to see the results of challenges by ratepayers of other comparable or competitor properties. It must also be recalled that, as a general rule, where the CCA process reduces an RV the reduction is retrospective, whereas where the CCA process increases an RV the increase is prospective only;[25] if a ratepayer considers that there is a risk of the VO concluding that his property is undervalued, therefore, the ratepayer's lack of challenge may be the result of waiting until close to the end of the list before commencing the process.

The tone of the list

Closely related to the comparable assessments valuation method is the concept of the "**tone of the list**".

In essence, a "tone" is said to form when the list assessments for a particular class of property have, through the process of CCA consideration and the passage of time, "settled down" to the point that

---

24 This is the effect of reg 5A of the Non-Domestic Rating (Alteration of Lists and Appeals) (England) Regulations 2009 (as amended).

25 Ibid, reg 14(7).

an established pattern of value has emerged. Where a tone exists, a new property in a relevant class can, on its entry in the list, be valued by reference to the tone, and the tone will stand as a (more or less) robust proxy for the property's RV.

The classic statement of how and when tones form is contained in the Lands Tribunal decision in *O'Brien v Harwood* RA/22/2002, per Mr P H Clarke FRICS at para 41:

> "*There are three stages leading to the establishment of tone of the list. At first, when a new rating list is put on deposit, entries will carry relatively little weight: they are opinions of value by the valuation officer, as yet unchallenged and untested by negotiation. Over time assessments will be challenged and agreed or determined by a valuation tribunal or this tribunal or accepted by lack of challenge. Finally a stage is reached where enough assessments have been agreed or determined or are unchallenged to establish a pattern of values, a tone of the list. The list is then said to have settled. Rents will be largely subsumed into assessments. At that stage rating surveyors will have little regard to rents and pay considerable attention to assessments. The position regarding tone of the list at any particular time is a question of fact. Where an assessment is challenged before a Tribunal the correct time for deciding whether a tone of the list has been established is immediately before the hearing*"

Where a list has settled and a tone has become established, that tone is a powerful basis for valuing a property. There are, however, several caveats to the reliability of a tone.

The first is that, as noted above, challenges to the content of a rating list may not be commenced until late in the life of a list, and in practice it can be many years after the closure of a list before its contents are finally settled.[26] Thus what may appear to be a settled tone is, in reality, merely pending resolution.

Even when a tone has been settled, and most appeals in respect of it resolved, it is relatively easy for tone to become disrupted. It sometimes happens that, late in a list and after a number of proposals have been settled or determined, valuers discover rental information of which none of the parties to the previous settlements or determinations were aware. If that rental evidence is contrary to the tone, and if the tone was settled in ignorance of the evidence, then it is usually the tone which must give way: the rent is, after all, a direct market signal, and opinions of value given in ignorance of a relevant market signal are undermined as a result.

Finally, it is an established principle of rating valuation that, while the purpose of the system is to provide a fair and equitable basis for a tax, nevertheless the valuer must not seek uniformity at the expense of accuracy. That principle was most famously stated by Scrutton LJ in *Ladies Hosiery and Underwear Ltd v West Middlesex Assessment Committee* [1932] 2 KB 679 at 688: "*the assessing authority should not sacrifice correctness to ensure uniformity, but, if possible, obtain uniformity by correcting inaccuracies rather than by making an inaccurate assessment in order to secure uniform error*". That principle was recently reaffirmed by the UK Supreme Court in *Hewitt (VO) v Telereal Trillium Ltd* [2019] 1 WLR 3262. It is sufficiently well-established as to be largely unchallengeable at this point, though one can understand the frustration of a ratepayer who finds it deployed against him to increase his RV above that of all of every other comparable property at a time when there is no mechanism for correcting those erroneously low assessments.

The rentals method and the comparable assessments method form the two principal means of valuing a property by comparison with other

---

[26] At the time of writing the author is aware of more than one 2010 list appeal which remain outstanding, despite that list having closed on 31 March 2017.

properties. How, though, does one approach the valuation of a property which has no comparables, either because similar properties are simply too far away to be useful, or because the property is unique in physical configuration or function? To value such properties, more arcane methods are required, and it is to those that we now turn.

CHAPTER NINE

THE RECEIPTS AND EXPENDITURE METHOD

In *Kingston Union v Metropolitan Water Board* [1926] AC 331, Viscount Cave LC said of the rating hypothesis that "*in applying that principle, so simple in appearance, to certain classes of hereditaments, great difficulties were encountered, and it was found necessary for rating experts and the Courts to have recourse to hypotheses of a more or less violent character*" [338). The particular hypothesis of a "violent character" that the Lord Chancellor was referring to was what is now known as the **receipts and expenditure** (or "R&E") method of valuation, and it is to that method that we now turn.

The premise of the R&E method is, in essence, that the amount of rent available to a tenant of a property is the amount of money "left over" from the receipts generated by the tenant's operation of its business from the property, after the deduction of (a) the expenses incurred in generating that revenue, including things like provision for repairs and the payment of relevant taxes (including rates), and (b) a sum to reward the tenant for its investment and risk in running the business (i.e. its profit).

It is thus possible, in suitable cases, to value a property by reference to the accounts of the actual business which is operating from the property. The obvious advantage of such an approach is that it can be applied to unique properties, or to properties of a kind which are seldom if ever let.

The method has its genesis in the 19th century, when it was known as the "profits" method (or the "revenue" method in Scotland). It evolved in response to the challenges of determining the rateable value of statutory or public service undertakings such as electricity networks, water-works, and railways. Such undertakings gave rise to two challenges for valuers: they were rarely if ever let, but were owner-occupied; and they regularly extended across more than one rating area, so that even if a part of a network happened to be let in a particular parish, that rental amount did not necessarily represent (or even give a clue as to) the proportion of the value of the whole which should be assigned to the parish.[27] The method was firmly established by the 1920s, when it was described and endorsed by the House of Lords on a number of occasions.

Today, the method is well-established as applicable to a range of property classes, including markets, cinemas, petrol stations, hotels, and a number of utility and industrial property types. Indeed, the last decade has seen the method grow in prominence: a combination of Upper Tribunal decisions and changes in VO practice has introduced the use of the method to classes which previously had been valued using either the contractor's basis or the shortened method. Thus the method has now been endorsed for use in valuing museums (following a line of Upper Tribunal decisions to which we will return), multi-story car parks (*BNPPDS v Ricketts (VO)* [2022] RA 255), and farm attractions (*Fryer v Cox (VO)* [2022 RA 357), amongst others.

27 That is a problem which valuers rarely have to grapple with now: by virtue of reg 6 of the Non-Domestic Rating (Miscellaneous Provisions) Regulations 1989, where a property comprises multiple hereditaments purely because it is located in more than one billing authority area, then it is valued as though it were a single hereditament, and that RV entered in the rating list for the billing authority which has the part which contains the component hereditament which appears to the VO to have the highest RV.

The method in outline

Broadly speaking, a valuer undertaking a valuation using the R&E method will go through the following steps in using the accounts to determine the property's RV:

- The **gross receipts** of the undertaking are determined, representing all income reasonably referable to the occupation of the hereditament in a given year.

- From those gross receipts are deducted the cost of purchases (i.e. those costs which are directly attributable to the production of a product, such as raw materials acquisition, transportation of parts, etc) to give the **gross profit** figure for the given year.

- From the gross profits are deducted the working expenses of the business (i.e. those costs which are incurred in the course of the ordinary operation of the business but which are not directly related to the production of a product). The figure produce by this operation is known in rating as the **divisible balance** (i.e. the net revenue figure which is to be divided between the hypothetical landlord and the hypothetical tenant)

- From the divisible balance is then taken an amount which is known as the **tenant's share**. This is the sum which reflects the hypothetical tenant's return on its invested capital, as well as the tenant's profits.

- Once the tenant's share is removed from the divisible balance, we are left with the **landlord's share**. This is the amount available to the hypothetical tenant to pay to rent the property, and indicates the likely RV of the hereditament.

Each of those elements can involve significant disputes between valuers, both as to the admissibility of an item of income or expenditure, and as to the quantum of admissible items. These disputes rarely give rise to issues of law, though it is not uncommon for points of valuation principle to be litigated as though they were points of law.

Detailed guidance on the application of each of these elements is contained in the 1997 Guidance Note on the R&E method, produced by the Joint Professional Institutions' Rating Valuation Forum.[28] Though now somewhat dated, the Note has nevertheless been treated by the Upper Tribunal as a reliable and authoritative statement of the approach which valuers should adopt.

We will now review some of the key issues which can arise at each of the stages.

Receipts

The determination of the receipts attributable to a business carried out from a hereditament can give rise to challenges.

The first point to note on this subject is that, while in most cases the starting point will be the accounts of the actual occupier, the R&E exercise is not concerned with valuing the actual occupier's business: it is concerned with identifying what the hypothetical tenant could make from its occupation, and thus what the hypothetical tenant can afford to give as rent.

Two main points flow from this.

First, it can require the actual occupier's accounts to be adjusted to reflect the receipts which the hypothetical tenant could achieve. If, for instance, the actual occupier has under-traded from a property for reasons peculiar

[28] The Joint Forum contained representatives from each of the RICS, the IRRV, the RSA, and the VOA, as well as the VOA's Scottish and Northern Irish equivalents.

to it, then its receipts may not reflect the fullness of the revenue potential which the hypothetical tenant could achieve. Conversely, if the income achieved by the actual occupier is inflated because of some special skill or industry possessed by the actual occupier and which is not possessed by the hypothetical tenant (bearing in mind that the actual occupier is a candidate for the hypothetical tenant), then the receipts may need to be adjusted downwards to reflect the position.

Secondly, where the occupier's business operates from a number of different properties, it is important that only those revenues referable to the subject hereditament are taken into consideration.

The notional receipts achievable by the hypothetical tenant, as distinct from those actually shown in the accounts for the actual occupier, are sometimes referred to by valuers as the property's "**fair maintainable trade**", though that is an expression more commonly used for the gross receipts when they are used as the basis of a shortened method valuation (see chapter 11).

In the early 20th century, a number of significant disputes arose as to whether or not statutory restrictions on the profits of the occupier were relevant to the gross receipts to be included in R&E valuations. These disputes typically arose in public utilities sectors, where the actual occupiers were public authorities whose fee structures were controlled by their governing Acts.

Broadly speaking, the authorities draw a distinction between two types of restriction. The first are statutory restrictions on the occupier's ability to generate revenue at all, e.g. a cap on the rates chargeable for the occupier's services. Such restrictions are relevant and should be reflected in the gross receipts, assuming of course that the restriction is one which would bind the property in anyone's hands (including the hypothetical tenant's). The second kind of restriction is one which does not affect the ability of the occupier to earn revenue as such, but rather restricts or controls what the occupier can do with the revenues once it has earned them.

The distinction was most clearly articulated by the House of Lords in *Port of London Authority v Orsett Union* [1920] AC 273, which concerned the statutory requirement for the Port of London to spend any and all surplus generated from its activities for the benefit of the Port itself. The House held that that restriction was irrelevant to the R&E valuation of the Port. Lord Dunedin put the point very pithily (299): "*sterility in earning profits is one thing, sterility in the disposing of profits is another. The former affects the value – the latter does not.*"

In any given year, any business may incur abnormal costs or receive one-off income, of the kind which the hypothetical tenant would not count on being able to receive in determining the level of its rental bid for the property. To mitigate against such one-off distortions, it is common for valuers to consider the accounts for several years leading up to the AVD, rather than focusing on the most recent set of accounts only. Considering three years' worth of accounts is common practice.

Importantly, however, valuers do not and should not simply average across the three years to arrive at the gross revenue. The risk of such an approach was explained very clearly by Viscount Hailsham LC in *Railways Assessment Authority v Southern Railway Co* [1936] AC 266 at 286:

> *"supposing one company had had net receipts during a quinquennium of one, two, three, four and five million pounds respectively, and another company during the same period had had receipts of five, four, three, two and one million pounds respectively, the average net receipts of each company would be the same, but it seems preposterous to suppose that the hypothetical tenant would give as much rent for the hereditaments in the second case as he would in the first."*

Rather than a mere averaging exercise, the valuer's task is to identify both the trends which the hypothetical tenant would take into account, and the abnormal items (of both income and expenditure) which the hypothetical tenant would disregard. The purpose of the exercise is to work out the basis on which the hypothetical tenant would bid: that involves the valuer putting himself in the hypothetical tenant's shoes, and deciding how the hypothetical tenant would have judged the future earning capacity of the property given the past accounts and as viewed from the AVD. As with many areas of valuation, the exercise involves as much art as it does science.

Cost of purchases and expenditure

The identification and quantification of the cost of purchases seldom gives rise to difficulty in R&E valuations, and is an element on which lawyers are seldom required to advise.

One area where consideration may need to be given is if the actual occupier, by virtue of its size and its wider portfolio of property holdings, can obtain economies of scale in the cost of its purchases which would not be available to the hypothetical tenant, or vice versa. In general, however, if the actual occupier's position in this respect depends on its wider holdings, there is nothing to prevent the assumption that the hypothetical tenant would itself be a company of similar character, if the market dynamics suggest that an entity of that kind would make the largest bid.

Turning to the expenditure category, there is a wide range of types of working expenses which are commonly seen in R&E valuations, and which have been accepted both by the tribunals and by the professional valuation bodies as admissible items for inclusion in a valuation. These can include:

a. Payments to staff, whether by way of salary or wage, including National Insurance contributions.

b. Arrangements for the supply of utilities or other equipment or services relevant to the operation of the business.

c. Non-domestic rates payments. It is now established that these are an admissible adjustment, and that the adjustment should be made as a line item of expenditure in the valuation (*Thomason v Roland (VO)* [1995] RA 255). The level of rates is that which existed at the AVD, i.e. the level of rates applicable given the RV of the property in the list prior to that for which the valuation is being undertaken. Thus for the 2023 list, the R&E will be based on the RV of the hereditament in the 2017 list. That removes what would otherwise be a challenging circularity in the analysis. It remains the case, though, that for properties valued on the R&E basis, a ratepayer's success in reducing its RV in one list will, all else being equal, produce an increase in its RV in the next list (because the rates as an item of deductible expenditure in the following list will have reduced, leaving a higher divisible balance). As a general proposition, the level of rates which the hypothetical tenant will assume to be payable will be the liability based on the RV actually shown in the list: the hypothetical tenant, being prudent, is unlikely to take into account any likelihood of a change in respect of the list extant at the AVD unless it is able to quantify both the likelihood of the change and the extent of the change (see *Fryer* at para 59 on this point).

d. Director's remuneration. This is an issue which has generated a significant amount of argument, usually in cases concerning the valuation of relatively small family-run businesses, where the modest amount of a director's salary can be significant given the relatively low overall values involved. The difficulty arises because the remuneration of the directors can arise in one (or both) of two ways – through the payment of a salary deductible as an item of expenditure, or through the profit and risk/reward allowance within the tenant's share. In *Redrose v Thomas (VO)* [2014] UKUT 311 (LC), the Upper Tribunal declined to include an expense line item for directors' pay, on the basis that the directors were fully remunerated via the tenant's share. Conversely, however, in *Fryer* a manager's salary was included as an expense, on the basis that the hypothetical tenant would need to employ one to cover the kind of work "in" the business that the actual occupiers undertook (para 66). The author suggests that what matters here is that the fullness of director remuneration is included somewhere – if no director's or manager's salary is allowed as an expense, then the directors' work in the business will need to be fully remunerated through the tenant's share, which may as a result be larger than it otherwise would have been.

e. Repairs to the hereditament itself. This is an admissible item of expenditure because, under para 2(1)(c) of Sch 6 to the 1988 Act, the tenant is responsible for keeping the property in the state of repair necessary to command the rent. For general, routine repairs, an annual deduction is the norm. For larger one-off repairs or replacements which the hypothetical tenant would envisage as falling due during the currency of its tenancy, it may be appropriate to adopt a sinking fund as a component of the valuation.

f. Repairs to the tenant's own plant and equipment.[29] Again, this can be envisaged as either an annual payment or as a sinking fund depending on the nature and extent of the anticipated liabilities.

g. Depreciation of the tenant's assets. Again, this can be done either by way of an expenditure item allowance to reflect the depreciation (and thus the reducing usefulness) of the assets, or by way of a sinking fund for the assets' eventual replacement. Care must however be taken to ensure that no double-counting

29 Which, by virtue of the established rules on the valuation of plant and machinery, are not to be treated as part of the hereditament for these purposes: Valuation for Rating (Plant and Machinery) (England) Regulations 2000.

occurs, as depreciation considerations and repair considerations can sometimes overlap.

The divisible balance

Once the allowable expenses and costs of purchases are identified and deducted from the gross revenue, what is left is the divisible balance, so called because it falls to be divided between the hypothetical landlord and the hypothetical tenant.

The in-principle approach to the divisible balance was set out by Viscount Hailsham LC in the *Southern Railway* case (282):

> *"The explanation for the use of the word "division" is probably to be found in the fact that it was the usual expression in rating law at the date of the Act, and that, if the amount which the tenant would require in order to induce him to take and operate the hereditaments is properly ascertained and deducted from the total net receipts, the result is to divide the net receipts fairly and justly between landlord and tenant, even though, in an extreme case, the landlord's share might be nothing at all. It is the rent which is to be estimated in such a way as to represent a fair and just division, and it is evident that the rent and nothing else is to be the landlord's share. When this is ascertained, the balance is the tenant's share of the net receipts. The "division" therefore is not to be an aliquot division on some unspecified basis, but is to be the result of a process involving the ascertainment of the landlord's share in the form of rent."*

In the same passage, Lord Hailsham emphasised that, in approaching the divisible balance, the relationship between the parties is one of landlord and tenant, and not that of joint venturers: the landlord has no interest in the success of the tenant's business as such, and the only return the landlord is entitled to receive is the rent itself.

It follows from Lord Hailsham's logic that the tenant's share is the first call on the divisible balance: otherwise, it is hard to see how the division could in any circumstances result in nothing being left for the landlord, which was a possibility that Lord Hailsham left open.

That being so, considerably more professional and judicial thought has been given to the calculation of the tenant's share, and little if anything is said about the landlord's share, which is simply what is left of the divisible balance once the tenant's share is removed.

Before looking at the approach to the tenant's share, it is worth observing that, if a property's expenses are greater than its revenue, so that it is loss-making for the hypothetical tenant, then the result is that the R&E method indicates a nominal value for the hereditament: the hypothetical tenant must be assumed to want to take the tenancy, but if the hypothetical tenant knows that in doing so it will make a loss, then the hypothetical tenant would not be prepared to take the property at a rent of anything more than £1 per annum. In *Telereal Trillium*, Lord Briggs JSC described this as a "*safety valve by which the necessary hypothesis that there is such a tenant is reconciled with a real world in which there may be, in fact, no demand for a letting of the property at all*" (para 64(b)).[30] Many of the disputes between the R&E and contractor's bases of valuation have arisen in contexts where the R&E method, applied strictly, has shown such a nominal RV.

30 Lord Briggs' speech in *Telereal Trillium* was a dissent, but his expression of the basic principles of rating in his para 64, including the principle cited here, is uncontroversial and does not conflict with the majority judgment of Lord Carnwath JSC.

The tenant's share

The determination of the tenant's share can, at least for larger and more valuable hereditaments, involve some of the most economically complex operations that arise in the rating context.

There are a number of possible approaches to determining the tenant's share, of varying complexity.

The most economically difficult method to adopt, and the one most likely to give a fully reasoned and robust figure, is to base the tenant's share on a percentage of the capital employed by the tenant in acquiring the staff, equipment etc it needs to run its business, as well as the working capital required to get the business up and running generally.

Again, the speech of Viscount Hailsham LC in *Southern Railway* contains helpful guidance on how to approach the hypothetical tenant's assumed acquisition of the required staff and equipment for the operation of its business (285):

> *"A further general observation occurs to me and that is that one may be led astray in the case of a railway undertaking by attempting too detailed or elaborate a personification of the hypothetical tenant. In the case of an ordinary house a rating authority may well visualize an ordinary citizen with all the usual desires, tastes and avocations of mankind as the tenant who is to pay the rent; but when we come to a railway undertaking in which vast sums have been invested and in which the share of the tenant's capital amounts to many millions it is apparent that the effort to visualize an actual tenant involves an almost impossible strain. In my opinion it would be a mistake to allow the percentage to be influenced by the largeness of the sum which the tenant is supposed to supply for capital, or by the difficulty of finding a tenant with such extensive means, or by the difficulty the tenant might find either in realizing his rolling stock and other chattels or in reinvesting*

> *so large an amount of capital on the expiration of his tenancy. Since the landlord is to be contemplated as a possible tenant, none of these considerations must be allowed to come in."*

It seems to the author that, if the solution to the difficulty of finding a person who is capable of providing the requisite equipment and expertise is to treat the actual occupier as the hypothetical tenant, then in most cases it will follow that the capital and equipment actually employed by the occupier must be reflected in the valuation, without adjustment towards some notional "better" business model which the hypothetical tenant may be said to adopt.

Once the amount of tenant's capital is determined, it is then necessary to determine the appropriate percentage. There are three components which need to be reflected in the percentage eventually adopted: interest, profit, and a risk allowance. For larger and more complex undertakings, these will generally be analysed separately; for smaller companies, a "blended" approach may be adopted, in which a single percentage figure is determined to reflect all three elements on a spot basis, without calculating the contribution of each.

Other approaches to the determination of the percentage of tenant's capital exist, which draw on wider company accounting concepts such as the ROCE (return on capital employed) achievable by relevant companies, or the WACC (weighted average cost of capital), which considers the rates applicable to both the company's debt and its equity. The detailed operation of these accounting methods is far beyond the scope of a textbook written by a lawyer for lawyers.

For the simpler classes of hereditament, it is relatively common for valuers not to engage in a detailed analysis of the occupier's capital position and expectations as to return, but instead to express the tenant's share as a straightforward percentage of the divisible balance. In *BNPPDS*, which concerned the valuation of multi-storey car parks on the R&E basis, the Upper Tribunal took into account the tenant's need for its share to reflect the three elements mentioned above (interest as a return on capital, profit and risk), and concluded that "*a balanced negotiation would always start, and often conclude at a 50% split between the two*" (para 59). The Tribunal thus applied a tenant's share of 50% of the divisible balance. In *Fryer*, the Upper Tribunal adopted a 75% tenant's share, reflecting the particularly high levels of risk associated with a farm attraction business such as that under consideration (para 87).

Whichever approach is adopted, the final stage in any R&E valuation – and in many ways the most important – is to "stand back and look". Has the application of the method produced a realistic, reasonable result? Are there any aspects of the parties' positions, or of the market, or of the property and its locality, which for whatever reason the method has not captured? The arithmetical result of the method must always be subject to this kind of professional judgment before the resultant valuation can be said to be truly reliable.

The "going concern" principle

As we saw in Part 1, it is often the case that, for rating valuation purposes, the hereditament is to be assumed to be vacant and to let, as a means of ensuring that the fullness of occupational value is realised from day one of the hypothetical tenancy.

When valuing property using the R&E method, however, the "vacant and to let" principle can hinder, rather than help, that objective: for businesses such as railways, the amount of staff and equipment required by the hypothetical tenant to commence trading is enormous, and if the property were vacant and to let on day one of the hypothetical tenancy, it could be many months before the hypothetical tenant could actually commence beneficial occupation.

To deal with that issue, it is common, in R&E valuations, to replace the "vacant and to let" principle with the "going concern" principle. The approach was explained by the Hong Kong Court of Final Appeal in

Hong Kong Electric Co Ltd v Commissioner for Rating and Valuation (2011) 14 HKCFAR 579, where Lord Millett NPJ held (para 187):

> *"valuing the [hypothetical tenant's] assets in situ does not give the sitting tenant an advantage because the assets must be treated as available in the same state to all potential tenants. The relevant hypothesis required ... is that the [hypothetical tenant] can acquire the necessary assets and staff without difficulty or interruption. The hypothesis is necessary in order to allow the [hypothetical tenant] (and every possible [hypothetical tenant]) the ability to take over the existing business with the existing assets in situ as a going concern without interruption and without cost."*

He added (para 199) that "*the so-called vacant and to let principle is not a free-standing rating hypothesis but a judicial extension ... and has no application where the tenement is valued as a going concern by the R&E method.*"

Socio-economic benefit: the museums cases

An issue which has generated a considerable degree of judicial consideration over the last decade or so is the treatment within R&E valuations of socio-economic benefit arising from an occupation.

While generally speaking properties valued on the R&E method will be occupied for a pure profit motive, this is not always the case, and the method is capable of being applied even where the occupier is not motivated by profit at all.

That has been the case for many decades. Indeed, the *Kinston Union* case with which the chapter started concerned a property the occupier of which was precluded by statute from making a profit, yet the R&E method was still applied.

Where properties are occupied by a local authority or a related body, and that occupation is not for profit, but in order to deliver a socio-economic benefit (whether it be cultural, touristic, educational, or in terms of general well-being) to the community, how if at all should that socio-economic benefit be quantified in the resultant valuation? That is an issue which was explored in a series of Upper Tribunal cases about the valuation of museums.

The first of the museums cases is one we have seen before: *Hughes (VO) v York Museums and Gallery Trust* [2017] RA 302. The case raised a significant number of issues, of which valuation was only part. It is one of those rating decisions that students of the subject should read carefully and fully. For our purposes, the issue in that case was the correct valuation approach to a series of hereditaments occupied by the YMGT. The ratepayer contended for the R&E method, despite the fact that in some of the cases the hereditaments were loss-making and the R&E method indicated a nominal value. The VO, by contrast, preferred the contractor's basis, despite the fact that the hereditaments comprised buildings which were in some cases many centuries old and which derived much of their interest from their histories (the Castle Museum, for instance, used to be a prison, and was the place where Dick Turpin spent his last night before his execution).

The Upper Tribunal rejected the application of the contractor's basis, for reasons which will be explored in the next chapter.

On the challenges of valuing a property occupied for other than a commercial profit motive, the Tribunal noted that properties could be occupied under statutory or moral duties; for charitable or quasi-charitable motivations such as the preservation of heritage assets; or the promotion of tourism or other socio-economic benefits to an area (para 124).

A variety of possible solutions to such a situation were identified by the Tribunal in the case law (para 125):

> *"there is no hard and fast rule where the nature of the hereditament lends itself to occupation by someone to whom it has more than a purely pecuniary value. A variety of different solutions to the problems of valuation have been adopted. The receipts and expenditure basis of valuation has sometimes been rejected altogether in favour of the contractor's basis (Gudgion; Scottish Exhibition Centre); sometimes it has been employed on the assumption that voluntary assistance or donations available to the actual tenant would continue to be available to the hypothetical tenant (Bluebell Railway); and sometimes an allowance or "overbid" has been assessed as representing the additional amenity value to the district which motives a public provider."*

Having reviewed the authorities, the Tribunal held (para 127) that:

> *"the fact that the receipts and expenditure method suggests a nominal or nil rateable value is not a reason for rejecting its use and resorting to the contractor's basis where it provides a reliable guide to the rent which would be offered for premises if let on the statutory hypothesis. On the contrary, in cases where premises cannot be occupied profitably, the receipts and expenditure method is often likely to be the better guide."*

The result was that the properties in question were valued on the R&E basis, resulting in one of the properties receiving an RV of £1.

The Upper Tribunal returned to the subject of museums valuation in *Hughes (VO) v Exeter City Council* [2020] RA 129, which concerned the Royal Albert Memorial Museum in Exeter. Once again, the VO contended for the application of the contractor's basis, which produced an RV of some £690,000, whereas it was common ground that if the R&E method were suitable, the indicated RV would be £1.

The decision of the Tribunal is magisterial and comprehensive, and repays careful reading in its entirety by anyone interested in valuation for rating. For present purposes, it is sufficient to note that the Tribunal once again rejected the contractor's basis, and preferred the R&E method despite it indicating a nominal value.

On the issue of a non-profit-motivated occupation, the Tribunal observed (para 164):

> *"The use of valuation judgment to assess the significance of factors such as socio-economic or cultural motivation, "a non-commercial aspect", affordability of rent, competing demands for the finite resources of a public authority is inescapable. That is so whether the valuer needs to make end allowances at stage 5 of the CB method, or adjustments to the outcome of an R & E valuation. An analysis of revenues and expenditure may assist the valuer in loss-making cases to weigh the significance of factors which are said to push the value upwards to judge whether the rateable value should ultimately be a positive figure (and, if so, how much) or a nil value. Judgments of this kind should be based upon evidence and valuation expertise and should be explained by the valuer ... However, we recognise that there may be some cases where the material available for such adjustments is justifiably limited and the expert can explain why that is so. But a difficulty in arriving at such figures should not necessarily mean that the valuation method is rejected. For example, the valuer may use more than one method to produce a range of figures to show how he has arrived at his final judgment."*

The Tribunal stressed that, in attempting to quantify socio-economic benefits, care must be taken to capture the value of the occupation to the occupier rather than to third parties or the wider community (para 225):

> *"although economic advantages for businesses and persons in a district, city or region which do not benefit the occupier of a hereditament financially may nevertheless hold some value for that occupier, they do not generally have as much value as those that do. The figures relied upon by [the VO] were essentially*

> *generalised benefits throughout the local economy and not sums of money receivable by the Respondent. Such benefits do not equate to value to the occupier resulting in an increase in the rent he would be prepared to pay, pound for pound. In the circumstances of this appeal, they do not hold the same value to the Respondent as revenues it may earn through its occupation of the hereditament. The Appellant did not suggest any method for expressing the valuation impact of socio-economic benefits on rental value, and we are not aware of any. But it is plain to us that these benefits, even if taken as a whole, would not represent value to the occupier of RAMM sufficient to overcome the economic disbenefit of having to subsidise the ongoing operating costs and to result in a positive rental value, even without taking into account issues of affordability. They certainly could not justify a rental value of the level which the VO seeks to advance in this appeal."*

The issue of socio-economic benefit came before the Tribunal for a third time, again on an appeal brought by the VO in respect of a museum, in *Allen (VO) v Tyne and Wear Archives and Museums* [2022] RA 277. In that appeal, the VO argued that it was possible to quantify socio-economic benefit, and that it had found a way to do so.

The Tribunal disagreed. The evidence presented by the VO sought to establish the socio-economic contribution of the museums to their communities; but the data did not identify the value of those community benefits to the hypothetical tenant, nor did it enable the valuer to quantify the effect on the hypothetical tenant's bid (para 112). The Tribunal went on to doubt whether a methodology to quantify those latter features was possible; there was certainly no methodology currently available to enable it to be done (para 113).

The result is that, at least as things stand, there is no mechanism for the inclusion of socio-economic benefit in R&E valuations, and the socio-economic aspect of an occupier's motivation must effectively be left out of account for valuation purposes when the R&E method is used.

The limitations of the method

The developments of the last decade have broadened the applicability of the R&E method, and it is now recognised as capable of use even where properties are occupied for a motive other than straightforward commercial profit. Indeed, the method is now firmly established as the approach of choice even in cases such as museums, which are far removed from a profit motive.

The R&E method depends, for its success, on the ability to produce reliable income and expenditure figures which are referable to the hereditament itself. If for any reason such figures are not available, then the reliability (and indeed the possibility) of the method is called into doubt. For a property which was newly-built at the AVD, for instance, there will be no past accounts on which the valuer can draw (though even in such cases it is possible to develop a R&E-style valuation using the business case and the operator's projections). There are also instances in which a hereditament is occupied for profit, but as part of a wider business: in some such cases it can be impossible reliably to assign any specific income or expenditure to the occupation of the subject hereditament in isolation. In such instances, another valuation approach must be adopted.

CHAPTER TEN

THE CONTRACTOR'S BASIS OF VALUATION

The last of the main valuation methods to consider, and the second of the indirect methods, is the **contractor's basis**.

The premise of the contractor's basis is that no tenant would pay more in rent for a property than it would have to pay each year in interest (either incurred on debts or foregone on investments) if it were to build an identical property from scratch. The contractor's basis thus involves valuing property by reference to the cost of both the buildings and the land which comprise the hereditament.

Valuation by reference to cost is a fraught business: it depends on the existence of an equivalence, or at least a relationship, between the cost of building something and the value of the resultant thing, and in many circumstances that relationship is either distorted, or non-existent. In such cases the contractor's basis may not be appropriate at all. This is a subject we will return to later in the chapter.

Like the R&E method, the contractor's basis was developed in the 19th century as a response to the challenge of valuing premises of a kind which were never let. Today, it is used mainly for large-scale industrial or commercial properties such as chemical works, airports, steel mills, oil refineries and shipbuilding yards, as well as other properties (especially public sector ones like schools and hospitals) which simply cannot be valued by any other means.

The contractor's basis in outline

The contractor's basis, in its modern iteration, involves five discrete valuation stages:

- Identify the build cost of the buildings, structures, and rateable plant and machinery which comprise the hereditament. This produces a figure known as the **estimated replacement cost.**

- Consider applying certain adjustments to the total stage 1 cost figure to reflect differences between the subject hereditament and a brand new building. This gives rise to the **adjusted replacement cost.**

- Add the value of the land element of the hereditament to the adjusted replacement cost. The figure produced at the end of stage 3 is known as the **effective capital value** of the hereditament.

- Decapitalise the effective capital value using a **decapitalisation rate** to arrive at an annualised figure representative of the interest incurred or foregone on the notional construction exercise.

- "**Stand back and look**", and make any final adjustments needed to arrive at an RV.

As with the R&E method, the Joint Professional Institutions' Rating Valuation Forum has produced a Guidance Note on the contractor's basis, the second edition of which was published by the RICS in 2007. Like its R&E counterpart, this Note is a recognised and authoritative source on the detail of the contractor's basis, and those seeking detailed advice on the individual components are referred to it.

Whenever the contractor's basis is applied, it must be kept in mind that the posited construction exercise is simply an aide to the valuation question, and the assumptions of the method must not be allowed to distort the question posed by the statutory hypothesis itself. This is a risk to be guarded against in any indirect valuation method, but is particularly acute in the case of the contractor's basis. As the Upper Tribunal warned in *York Museums and Gallery Trust* (para 130):

> *"it is important not to allow an assumption about the relationship between cost and value to become an assumption about the behaviour of the parties to the notional letting. In particular it should not be assumed that in practice either the landlord or the tenant would consider reproducing the hereditament or could do so. As the Lands Tribunal (T Hoyes FRICS and PH Clarke FRICS) emphasised when rejecting too literal an application of the contractor's basis in Monsanto plc v Farris [1998] RA 107, 141: "an alternative hereditament ... is neither built nor valued, it is a total fiction and as such it should not be dressed in the clothes of supposed reality, because that produces even greater unreality and an array of problems.""*

A method of last resort?

The contractor's basis is often referred to, both by valuers and by the tribunals, as the valuation "method of last resort": if another method, such as rentals or R&E, is available, then that is generally preferable to the contractor's basis.

The reason for regarding the contractor's basis in this way was explained by the Upper Tribunal in *York Museums and Gallery Trust* at para 131:

> *"Although theoretically sound, in practice the method can involve the making of allowances or adjustments with little evidence to support them which may appear arbitrary and unjustifiable and which, though small in themselves, can have a substantial effect on the end value."*

In *Acenden*, the Upper Tribunal agreed that the contractor's basis was a method of last resort, "*which is tolerated as a means of establishing the annual letting value of property only because no better method can be found for some hereditaments*" (para 90).

In the *RAMM* case, the Tribunal stressed that the "last resort" principle should not be taken too far (para 76):

> *"We note that the CB has sometimes been described as a "method of last resort" to reflect its potential weaknesses. But the R & E and CB methods are both indirect methods of valuation. There is no legal hierarchy as between the two."*

Nevertheless, recent decisions have tended, when faced with a choice between the R&E method and the contractor's basis, to prefer the former, and the author suggests that the R&E method is emerging as the more methodologically reliable of the two indirect valuation approaches.

We will now consider the five stages in turn.

Stage 1 – estimated replacement cost

Stage 1 of the process involves calculating what, at the AVD, it would have cost to have built a property like the hereditament as it was on the material day.

There are, broadly, two approaches in practice to this exercise.

The first is to cost the construction of the hereditament exactly as it stands. The exercise begins by identifying the rateable aspects of the property, and then moves to costing them. The costing will need to include all of the costs which would in practice be incurred to achieve the construction of such a replica, including things like design costs and site staffing and supervision costs. It is not simply the bricks and mortar which must be costed, but the whole of the exercise of assembling them into a replica building.

The costings are usually done by considering unit costs as they stood at the AVD.

Where the hereditament was constructed recently, then the actual costs data may be available to the valuer, and that can provide a helpful guide as to the stage 1 ERC. Care must be taken, however, to exclude any non-rateable elements wrapped up in the build costs, and to ensure that the elements of the costs are adjusted to the AVD appropriately (the market in wages may for instance have shifted in a different way to the market for raw materials, so that different indices need to be used).

The second approach is not to seek to cost the actual hereditament, but instead to cost what valuers call a "**modern substitute**". This tends to be adopted for older hereditaments, where technology and business practices have moved on so that, in reality, no-one seeking to achieve the hereditament's functions would replicate the hereditament itself, but would build something smaller or more efficient. While the modern substitute approach has its advantages, it is particularly important to remember that the goal is to value the hereditament itself, and not to value some other notional building. The modern substitute approach is nothing more than a tool to assist in establishing the amount which the hypothetical tenant might pay in rent for the actual hereditament.

The stage 1 process is, in essence, a quantity surveying exercise, and rating surveyors often receive input from other property professionals in estimating the relevant build costs. From a litigation perspective, it is important that, if non-rating input is sought in this way, it is presented to the tribunal in a manner capable of carrying meaningful weight in the overall valuation decision. In *Nelson Plant Hire Ltd v Bunyan (VO)* [2023] RA 29, the Upper Tribunal noted that the reliability of the contractor's basis, and its status as the method of last resort, was exacerbated "*where a significant component of the contractor's basis valuation is reliant on the views of others who did not give evidence and whose conclusions were simply adopted by [the valuer] without consideration of the underlying evidence on which they were based*" (para 112).

Stage 2 – adjusted replacement cost

The stage 1 ERC is produced by reference to a building which, at the AVD, is brand new. In many cases, however, the hereditament itself will not be brand new. The purpose of stage 2 is to adjust the ERC to reflect the actual condition of the hereditament as compared to the notional newly-built property costed at stage 1.

Valuers tend to refer to the deficiencies of the hereditament as compared to the stage 1 brand new property using the language of "obsolescence". There are three broad ways in which a property may be "obsolete" to a greater or lesser degree for these purposes: **physical obsolescence**, which arises from considerations like the costs associated with the age of the building; **technological obsolescence**, which arises where the way in which the hereditament operates to achieve its purpose is out of date and inefficient (the building may be configured for a process which uses far more energy than would be the case for a building configured to use the most up-to-date processes, for instance; or parts of the building which were necessary when it was constructed may have become redundant because of technological advances); and **functional obsolescence**, which relates to deficiencies in the design of the building itself.

As will be apparent, there is a degree of overlap between these categories, and care must be taken not to "double count" a deficiency through multiple overlapping allowances, nor to miss out a deficiency which falls through the gaps between the categories.

In the context of industrial buildings, valuers have widely adopted an approach to stage 2 allowances known as the "Monsanto scale", after the approach adopted by the Lands Tribunal in the chemical plant contractor's basis valuation appeal of *Monsanto plc v Farris* [1998] RA 107. Having heard detailed evidence on the depreciation of physical assets, the Tribunal in *Monsanto* adopted an approach whereby physical obsolescence was reflected in an allowance of 0.5% per year for the first 10 years of a building's life, and 1% per year for every additional year up to 50 years old. That scale can be useful in the right circumstances; but it is categorically <u>not</u> appropriate to all buildings. The Upper Tribunal made that clear in *York Museums*, in rejecting the use of the Monsanto scale for the hereditaments there under consideration (para 187):

> *"Allowances employed in the valuation of a post-war chemical works have no relevance to historic listed buildings used as museums and art galleries. The limitations of the scale were acknowledged by [the VO's witness] when he accepted that it did not differentiate between a building of 50 years old and one of 1,050 years old – both would attract an allowance of 50%. That the scale stops at 50 years is not the result of any valuation principle but simply a reflection of the age of the buildings with which the original Monsanto proceedings were concerned. We do not criticise the widespread adoption of the Monsanto allowances in contractor's basis settlements relating to industrial buildings, but their use in industrial settlements lends them no additional credibility or relevance as a tool for valuing other types of building."*

A final point to bear in mind here is that, if the modern substitute approach were adopted at stage 1, a lot of what would otherwise be covered by stage 2 obsolescence allowances will already have been reflected in the adoption of a cheaper, smaller modern substitute for determining the ERC. Again, the valuer must guard against double-counting.

Stage 3 – land value

The land value with which the valuer is concerned at stage 3 is the AVD open market capital value of the land component of the hereditament.

Broadly speaking, calculating this value involves two stages. The first is to determine the value of the land in its undeveloped state. This is usually done by seeking market evidence of the sales of comparable cleared sites. It must be recalled, however, that the hereditament is limited to use for its existing mode or category of occupation: the value sought at this stage is therefore the value of undeveloped land which has permission for use for the relevant mode or category, and without reflecting any development value inherent in the cleared land for other more lucrative uses.

The second stage is to adjust that undeveloped land value to reflect the impact of the buildings which are actually on it: the presence of buildings affected by obsolescence will often be to reduce the value of the land on which those buildings sit, as well as reducing the value of the buildings themselves. For that reason, it is common practice to apply the stage 2 ARC allowances to the undeveloped land value, in order to arrive at the value of the land component of the hereditament.

This adjustment is known as an "Ebdon allowance", after the decision of the Lands Tribunal in *Imperial College of Science and Technology v Ebdon (VO)* [1984] RA 213.[31] The Tribunal described and accepted the logic of the valuers as to the need for such an allowance: "*if the site cleared of all buildings is worth over £6.25 million when it could accommodate new buildings costing over £20 million, it must be worth less when developed with the existing buildings which are agreed to be less valuable*" (230). The Tribunal emphasised that the amount of the Ebdon allowance was a

[31] There was a subsequent appeal to the Court of Appeal against this decision; but that related solely to the question of the stage 4 decapitalisation rate, and the Tribunal's reasoning on the stage 3 approach was unchallenged.

matter of fact in any given case: in the circumstances of that appeal it was reasonable for the allowance to be the same as the stage 2 allowance made for the obsolescence of the existing buildings, but there was no reason in principle why a different allowance should not be adopted if the evidence justified it.

Stage 4 – decapitalisation

The purpose of stage 4 is to express the ECV as an annualised figure, to reflect the interest incurred or foregone per annum which the hypothetical tenant would consider in its assessment of its rental bid for the hereditament. The decapitalisation rate (often called the "decap rate" by practitioners) is governed by two main considerations: the cost of capital (in terms of both debt and equity), and a consideration formerly known as the "Denning Discount" (from the judgment of Lord Denning MR in *Cardiff Corp v Williams (VO)* [1973] RA 46). The Denning Discount is necessary because the contractor's basis tells the hypothetical tenant what he would have to pay per annum to acquire the hereditament on a freehold basis: once the construction and acquisition debt is cleared, he will have a valuable and unencumbered capital asset. The hypothetical tenant, by contrast, is renting the property, and at the end of his term will be left with nothing. That factor is reflected in contractor's basis valuations through the level at which the stage 4 rate is set.

Historically, this is an issue which generated very considerable controversy, and many days of tribunal time were spent determining the correct decap rate for the property under consideration.

In recognition of that difficulty, the legislature intervened, and since 1990 the decap rate to be used in contractor's basis valuations has been prescribed.

The rates are contained in reg 2 of the Non-Domestic Rating (Miscellaneous Provisions) (No 2) Regulations 1989, which prior to the compilation of a new list is amended to show the decap rates to apply to that new list.

For the 2023 list, the Government decided not to alter the rates which had applied to the 2017 list. Thus for defence, education and healthcare hereditaments, the decap rate is 2.6%, and for all other properties the rate is 4.4% (reg 2(2F)). The difference reflects the generally cheaper borrowing rates available to large government departments.

Stage 5 – stand back and look

As with the R&E method, the final, "stand back and look" stage of the contractor's basis is in many respects the most important: this is the point at which valuer judgment really comes into play, and the result of the prior 4 stages is scrutinised for its reasonableness.

Indeed, in many ways the stand back and look process is even more important in the context of the contractor's basis than it is in other forms of valuation.[32] It is well-established that the first four stages of the contractor's basis indicate a cap on rental value: the hypothetical tenant would pay no more for the hereditament than the annualised cost of starting from scratch. But the hypothetical tenant may very well pay less.

There may be factors which would bear on the higgling of the market for the property, but which have not been captured by stages 1-4. It would be impossible to attempt a comprehensive list of the sort of allowances which have been made at stage 5. In case examples assist, in *Semlogistics Milford Haven Ltd v Webb (VO)* [2018] RA 200, which concerned an oil storage depot, a stage 5 allowance was made to reflect the increased maintenance and dredging costs associated with the hereditament as

32 In *Nelson Plant Hire*, the absence of any stage 5 narrative in an expert's valuation report was something which the Tribunal considered to cast doubt on the valuation overall (para 112).

compared with a modern substitute (para 185); and in *British Car Auctions Ltd (t/a/ Blackbushe Airport Ltd) v Hazell (VO)* [2015] RA 108, a 30% stage 5 allowance was applied to the valuation of an airfield to account for a range of disabilities, including the existence of a bridleway which crossed the airfield, as well as difficulties in erecting additional hangers next to the airfield.

In the *RAMM* case, the Upper Tribunal added that "*the Tribunal might be satisfied that a substantial reduction should be made at stage 5 because the hypothetical tenant genuinely could not afford, or justifiably would not be prepared to pay, the figure resulting from stage 4*" (para 145). That can be demonstrated by rental evidence,[33] or by the result of a R&E valuation, for instance.

For a while, following the Upper Tribunal decision in *Allen v English Sports Council* [2009] RA 289, it was thought that issues around willingness to pay were subsumed into the statutory decap rate at stage 4, and so did not warrant a stage 5 allowance. However, in *RAMM* the Upper Tribunal confirmed that that view was erroneous and should not be followed: the decap rate is concerned simply with identifying and prescribing the cost of capital, and is unconcerned with any of the other matters which have conventionally fallen to be considered at stage 5 (including affordability) (para 147).

---

33 It can be the case that some rental evidence exists in contractor's basis cases, and while that evidence is usually insufficient to enable a rentals valuation to take place, it can still be used as a sense check on the contractor's basis valuation at stage 5.

The limitations of the contractor's basis

As will be abundantly clear by now, the contractor's basis derives value by considering cost, and its reliability is wholly dependent on there existing a demonstrable relationship between the cost of building a property and its resultant rental value.

In many cases, however, the value of a property has little if anything to do with the cost of building it, and in such cases the contractor's basis is un unreliable guide to value. The example used by the author when teaching pupil barristers is that of Hampton Court Palace – if a brick-for-brick replica of the palace were to be built nearby, that replica would not approach the value of the original, because much of the value of the original comes from its history: Henry VIII never slept in the replica. The value of the palace thus bears no relationship to the cost of its reproduction.

The limitations of the contractor's basis were explored in the museums cases which we considered in the previous chapter.

The basic difficulty with the contractor's basis in such cases was explained in *York Museums* at para 184:

> *"At the most fundamental level we can see no justification in the case of historic buildings used as museums or visitor attractions for the assumption underlying the contractor's basis that notional costs of construction bear some consistent relationship to rental value. Such buildings are often, as the evidence demonstrates, inherently unprofitable yet would be very expensive to construct either in their original form or as a modern substitute. The statutory rating hypothesis requires the assumption of a letting of expensive and inefficient historic buildings on terms which the evidence suggests could not be achieved in reality; it does not require that the commercial viability of the enterprise or the risks of assuming responsibility for the maintenance of such premises be ignored. Nor does the*

> *statutory hypothesis permit the making of an assumption, without evidence, that the sort of tenant who might take a tenancy of an historic building for use as a museum would have external sources of revenue sufficient to enable the payment of a commercial rent where the purpose for which they wish to occupy the premises themselves is likely to be loss making."*

In *RAMM*, the contractor's basis was rejected primarily because the rent which it indicated was, in reality, entirely unachievable by a local authority occupier (the only possible hypothetical tenant) subject to legal restrictions on local government spending (para 240).

In the light of the museums cases, and the resultant application of the R&E method to inherently unprofitable hereditaments, the role of the contractor's basis is now considerably more circumscribed than it was.

Other cost-based valuation approaches

So far, we have considered cases where the whole of the hereditament is valued on the contractor's basis. That is not, however, the only way in which cost can be relevant to valuation.

It is not uncommon for discrete parts of a property to be valued by reference to cost, even if the remainder of the hereditament is valued on some other basis. In *Berry v Iceland* [2015] RA 201, for instance, the Upper Tribunal used a costs-based approach to value the bespoke air handling system in a supermarket.[34]

---

[34] The logically prior question of whether the air handing system was rateable at all was eventually determined on appeal by the Supreme Court; but the valuation approach to be adopted in the event that the system was rateable was not disturbed on appeal.

An interesting issue in such cases is whether the costs-based component of such a valuation is required to use the statutory decap rate to annualise the identified cost.

In *Iceland*, the Upper Tribunal appeared to have accepted that the statutory decap rate was mandated in valuations of that kind. The position was revisited by the Upper Tribunal in *Bunyan (VO) v Acenden*, however, and in that case the Upper Tribunal held that the statutory rates were mandated only where a "full" contractor's basis valuation is undertaken, as opposed to valuing a non-severable aspect of a hereditament by reference to its cost. The Upper Tribunal recognised that a part of a hereditament could be valued on the contractor's basis, and that in such a scenario the statutory decap rate had to be used; but its use was mandated only where the part in question would be capable of having a RV of its own if it were to be separately assessed (para 99). *Acenden* was concerned with the valuation of the category B fit out of a Grade A office building, and self-evidently the tenant's fit out of such a property cannot comprise a hereditament of its own.

The *Acenden* approach to this issue is not without its difficulties. It sits uncomfortably with the approach of the Tribunal in earlier cases such as *Iceland* and *Dorothy Perkins Retail Ltd v Casey* [1994] RA 391; and in any event the Tribunal rejected a costs-based valuation of the category B fit out anyway, preferring an alternative valuation approach. The approach also opens the door to argument and litigation about the rate at which the cost of elements of a hereditament should be decapitalised, which is precisely what the statutory rates are intended to avoid. Nevertheless, the current position is that, where a non-severable part of a hereditament is valued by reference to its cost, the valuer is not required to use the statutory rates to determine the annualisation of that cost, but can adopt whatever rate seems appropriate given the evidence.

CHAPTER ELEVEN

OTHER METHODS

The preceding chapters have described the main modern methods of valuation. This chapter considers the handful of other methods, or greater or lesser persuasiveness, which may be encountered from time to time.

The shortened method

Of the methods in this chapter, by far the most important is what is known as the **shortened method**.

The premise of the shortened method is that, for certain classes of property, there is a relationship between the rent which an occupier would be prepared to pay, and the amount of gross receipts which the occupation of the property is able to generate. If such a relationship is established, then the valuer who knows the gross receipts generated by a property is able to apply the relevant percentage to derive the rent.

As will be apparent from this brief description, the shortened method, though often spoken of in the same breath as the R&E method, is in fact a form of comparative valuation. Unlike the rental method, however, the point of the comparison is not to enable a unit price to be applied, but to identify and enable a percentage of gross receipts to be identified.

The shortened method has the advantage of being much quicker and easier to apply than a full R&E valuation – once the relevant percentage of receipts is identified, then it is a quick and straightforward matter to value a property in the relevant class. All that is required is to identify the fair maintainable trade (i.e. the gross revenue achievable by the hypothetical tenant), and apply the percentage.

As a valuation approach, the shortened method has long had its judicial detractors. In *Hoare (VO) v National Trust* (1999) 77 P&CR 366, the VO had suggested that the shortened method could be used to derive the value of the Trust's "overbid" for securing the tenancy of a property the occupation of which would be consistent with the Trust's statutory objectives. Schiemann LJ declined to give a firm view on this issue, as it was not strictly necessary to resolve the case. In those circumstances, he said (384):

> *"I content myself with recording my total inability as at present advised to understand the theoretical justification for arriving at the amount of the overbid by starting at the gross receipts figure rather than a profit figure. The fact that one can adjust the percentage of that gross receipts figure in order to arrive at the hypothetical rent does not detract from the arbitrariness of starting with that gross figure. Moreover the amount of the percentage reduction seems to me equally arbitrary. The resulting valuations give a wholly misleading picture of scientific rigour. One suspects that what the valuer does is to use his evaluation of all the facts of the case and arrive at an intuitive figure and then build a theoretical structure to justify it. I cannot see any rational hypothetical tenant … using that theoretical structure to arrive at the amount of his overbid in his negotiations with the hypothetical landlord. Nor can I see the hypothetical landlord having such calculations in mind."*

An inauspicious start for any valuation method.

The limitations of the method have been expanded on in recent Upper Tribunal cases.

In *BNPPDS*, which concerned multi-storey car parks, the Upper Tribunal stressed the conditions which needed to be in place before the shortened method could be regarded as a reliable indicator of value (para 49):

> *"Given that we lack the necessary evidence for a valuation by rental comparison it follows that in this instance the shortened method is inappropriate, this latter method being a derivation of the former. It is obvious, as Mr Wilcox pointed out, that the shortened method by its nature cannot fully take account of the different operational costs of different hereditaments. Although we appreciate the convenience of the shortened method it seems to us that distilling all of the attributes, trading prospects and locational aspects of a property into a single numeric factor requires a great deal of insight and could be prone to errors of judgement. Valuation of car parks by means of a percentage of receipts is, in our view, only appropriate after a rigorous analysis of a proper sample of rental transactions or in situations where there is already a settled tone derived from a comparison of rents and FMT."*

Similar concerns were raised in *Fryer* about the use of the method for the valuation of farm attractions (para 82):

> *"We take the view that the use of the shortened method is ill-advised in the absence of rental evidence or full R & E valuations on which to base the selection of the appropriate percentage. We have already noted a lack of reliable rental evidence in this case and neither party has adduced any R & E valuations of comparable properties in support of their case."*

In *Tyne and Wear*, the Tribunal urged "*extreme caution*" in using the shortened method, unless there was "*a rigorous analysis of the available rental evidence, or a significant number of assessments agreed on the full receipts and expenditure basis*" (para 105).

Two key points emerge from these decisions.

The first is that, for the shortened method to be reliable, there must be a well-established understanding of the relationship between rents and fair maintainable trade for the relevant class. By definition, that understanding cannot flow from the use of the shortened method itself: it must be achieved using one of the other valuation methods. The Tribunal has endorsed the rentals, tone of the list, and R&E methods for this purpose. Only once a sufficient number of properties have been valued using other methods, and only if a consistent pattern emerges as to the relationship between the FMT and the rent, can the shortened method be considered.

The second point relates to the role of cost. The shortened method derives rent from an analysis of revenue for a given class of property. But unless the costs of operating properties in that class bear a relationship to revenue as well, the method may be misleading.

This is best illustrated by an example. Take two properties in a relevant class. Property A generates a FMT of £100,000, incurs £50,000 of expenditure to achieve that revenue, and is rented in the open market for £10,000 per annum, i.e. 10% of FMT. Property B is in the same class. It generates a FMT of £150,000. But because of the particular characteristics of this property (its location or layout, say), the expenditure which must be incurred to realise that revenue is £120,000. The logic of the shortened method would suggest that the rental value of Property B would be £15,000 per annum (10% of FMT). From an economic perspective, however, such a result is absurd: no rational business would pay a higher rent for Property B, which generates net receipts of £30,000, than it would for Property A, which generates net receipts of £50,000.

The shortened method is thus unreliable in those cases where there is variability as to the proportion of the FMT which goes on to become net revenue.

Despite those shortcomings, the shortened method is the established valuation approach for some classes of property, such as bingo halls. It is also used occasionally as a "sense check" on the results of properties valued using the R&E or contractor's basis, to see whether the results of those methods fit with the value patterns for comparable properties.

The author's view is that the future of the method is precarious. No other valuation method has received such robust criticism from the expert tribunals and courts, and while the shortened method is cheap and easy to apply, valuers should generally be wary of taking the quick and cheap option, particularly when producing expert valuation reports for consideration by the tribunals.

Inter-list comparability

Where a property is already shown in a rating list, then its RV in that list can on occasion be used to inform its RV in the next rating list. This is sometimes referred to as valuation by **inter-list comparability** or relativity.

This is, in effect, a form of valuation by indexation: take the RV in the old list, adjust it by the movement in the relevant market from one AVD to the next, and that will give an indication of the RV for the new list.

Indexation over anything more than a few months is a notoriously unreliable exercise, and indexation across the years between rating lists is a crude approach at best. It can, however, be helpful as a sense check: if a property valued on (say) the contractor's basis finds its RV increasing wildly from one list to the next, when other properties in the same class and broad locality have seen more modest rises, then that suggests that something may have gone wrong with the contractor's basis valuation.

The Upper Tribunal has considered valuation by inter-list relativity on a number of occasions. In *Lamb (VO) v Minards* [1974] RA 153, the Lands Tribunal considered entries in previous lists to be of no direct assistance in assessing RVs for new lists, though acknowledging that the relativities between properties in one list may be of "*some help*" in assessing the relativities to apply in the new list. In such circumstances, it was open to the VO to show that not only the absolute values, but also the inter-hereditament relativities, had changed over the period from one list to the next (161). In *Barnard & Barnard v Walker (VO)* [1975] RA 383, this was described as a rebuttable presumption that the relativities in values between properties in one list would remain consistent in the next list.

That presumption will be rebutted where inter-list comparisons show too high a degree of variability. In *Lidl (UK) GmbH v Ryder (VO)* [2014] 23, for instance, Mr Rose FRICS rejected a contention that the relationship between the RVs or a number of Lidl stores between the 2005 and 2010 rating lists was a guide to value, "*in the light of the fact that the percentage increases in the value of Lidl's properties in the 2010 list varied very considerably from store to store*" (para 81). The same conclusion was reached in *Lamb v Go Outdoors,* with Mr McCrea FRICS explaining (para 82):

> *"The variance between the 2005 and (current but in many cases appealed) 2010 assessments was notable. Some had increased, some decreased, and some remained static. I accept Mr Cohen's point that this variance and the parameters of increase or decrease may alter as and when each assessment is agreed or determined by a Tribunal. To limit the amount by which the assessment of the appeal property should alter, by reference to the change between rating lists of other assessments which themselves are subject to appeal, and in doing so then possibly affect the ultimate result of those other appeals, would in my judgement be to let the tail wag the dog."*

In such circumstances, the *Barnard & Barnard* presumption was rebutted (para 83).

Statutory prescription

For many years, certain classes of property (in particular in the public utilities sector) were not valued as such, but rather had their RVs assigned to them by **prescription**.

Today, there are two mechanisms by which a property's RV, or an element of it, may be prescribed.

The first is contained in para 2(8) of Sch 6 to the 1988 Act. That provision empowers the Secretary of State to prescribe assumptions which are to be made in the application of the statutory hypothesis to hereditaments of prescribed classes. This mechanism is not used for prescribing RVs as such, but rather for prescribing aspects of a valuation: it is para 2(8) that is the source of the regulations around the treatment of plant and machinery, for instance. Para 2(11) makes clear that the Secretary of State can make prescriptions by reference to such factors as he sees fit.

The second mechanism is contained in para 3 of Sch 6. That empowers the Secretary of State to disapply the rating hypothesis altogether for specified classes of hereditaments, and instead to have those hereditaments valued in accordance with prescribed rules. Again, the Secretary of State can in making regulations under para 3 consider such factors as he sees fit (para 3(3)).

There has been a strong move against prescribed valuations for hereditaments in the 21st century, and para 3 was repealed by s. 69 of the Local Government Act 2003. S. 69 has not yet been brought into force, however. The current position, therefore, is that para 3 prescription is still legally available to the Secretary of State, though as a policy preference it is not currently used, and there are no classes of hereditament for which a para 3 prescription is in place.

Spot valuation

As has been mentioned several times already in this book, valuation is more an art than a science, and valuer judgment must always be applied to the determination of the RV of any property.

The ultimate expression of this is the **spot valuation**, which is essentially a valuer's instinctive view of the value of a property as informed by his professional experience and expertise.

This is not a method which is used in isolation. But the valuer's instinct is not to be discounted out of hand, and if the result of any given valuation method causes the valuer professional discomfort, or simply "feels" wrong, then this is something which much be grappled with and not simply ignored in favour of more apparently scientific approaches. The author recalls a learned Judge observe of such an approach that "it may be a finger in the air, but it is an expert finger".

Future methods

The methods of valuation set out in this book are those which are currently in use. Each and every one of them is of some degree of antiquity, and has been established and refined through consideration and application by valuers both in private and public practice, as well as by the specialist rating tribunals.

It does not follow, however, that the class of methods of valuation for rating is closed. Rating surveying is an ingenious profession, and valuers often find approaches to novel situations which can take even the most seasoned rating lawyers by surprise. As long as the method is targeted at answering the question which the statutory hypothesis poses, then it is admissible. Who can say what new methods of valuation will emerge in the coming years and decades, in response to changes in the market and developments in technology and surveying practice? Rating may be ancient, but it is still exciting!

MORE BOOKS BY LAW BRIEF PUBLISHING

A selection of our other titles available now:-

'A Practical Guide to the Independent School Standards – September 2023 Edition' by Sarah McKimm
'A Practical Guide to Estate Administration and Crypto Assets' by Richard Marshall
'A Practical Guide to Managing GDPR Data Subject Access Requests – Second Edition' by Patrick O'Kane
'A Practical Guide to Parental Alienation in Private and Public Law Children Cases' by Sam King QC & Frankie Shama
'Contested Heritage – Removing Art from Land and Historic Buildings' by Richard Harwood QC, Catherine Dobson, David Sawtell
'The Limits of Separate Legal Personality: When Those Running a Company Can Be Held Personally Liable for Losses Caused to Third Parties Outside of the Company' by Dr Mike Wilkinson
'A Practical Guide to Transgender Law' by Robin Moira White & Nicola Newbegin
'A Practical Guide to 'Stranded Spouses' in Family Law' by Mani Singh Basi
'A Practical Guide to Residential Freehold Conveyancing' by Lorraine Richardson
'A Practical Guide to Pensions on Divorce for Lawyers' by Bryan Scant
'A Practical Guide to Challenging Sham Marriage Allegations in Immigration Law' by Priya Solanki
'A Practical Guide to Digital Communications Evidence in Criminal Law' by Sam Willis
'A Practical Guide to Legal Rights in Scotland' by Sarah-Jane Macdonald
'A Practical Guide to New Build Conveyancing' by Paul Sams & Rebecca East
'A Practical Guide to Defending Barristers in Disciplinary Cases' by Marc Beaumont
'A Practical Guide to Inherited Wealth on Divorce' by Hayley Trim
'A Practical Guide to Practice Direction 12J and Domestic Abuse in Private Law Children Proceedings' by Rebecca Cross & Malvika Jaganmohan

'A Practical Guide to Confiscation and Restraint' by Narita Bahra QC, John Carl Townsend, David Winch
'A Practical Guide to the Law of Forests in Scotland' by Philip Buchan
'A Practical Guide to Health and Medical Cases in Immigration Law' by Rebecca Chapman & Miranda Butler
'A Practical Guide to Bad Character Evidence for Criminal Practitioners by Aparna Rao
'A Practical Guide to Extradition Law post-Brexit' by Myles Grandison et al
'A Practical Guide to Hoarding and Mental Health for Housing Lawyers' by Rachel Coyle
'A Practical Guide to Psychiatric Claims in Personal Injury – 2nd Edition' by Liam Ryan
'Stephens on Contractual Indemnities' by Richard Stephens
'A Practical Guide to the EU Succession Regulation' by Richard Frimston
'A Practical Guide to Solicitor and Client Costs – 2nd Edition' by Robin Dunne
'Constructive Dismissal – Practice Pointers and Principles' by Benjimin Burgher
'A Practical Guide to Religion and Belief Discrimination Claims in the Workplace' by Kashif Ali
'A Practical Guide to the Law of Medical Treatment Decisions' by Ben Troke
'Fundamental Dishonesty and QOCS in Personal Injury Proceedings: Law and Practice' by Jake Rowley
'A Practical Guide to the Law in Relation to School Exclusions' by Charlotte Hadfield & Alice de Coverley
'A Practical Guide to Divorce for the Silver Separators' by Karin Walker
'The Right to be Forgotten – The Law and Practical Issues' by Melissa Stock
'A Practical Guide to Planning Law and Rights of Way in National Parks, the Broads and AONBs' by James Maurici QC, James Neill et al
'A Practical Guide to Election Law' by Tom Tabori
'A Practical Guide to the Law in Relation to Surrogacy' by Andrew Powell
'A Practical Guide to Claims Arising from Fatal Accidents – 2nd Edition' by James Patience
'A Practical Guide to the Ownership of Employee Inventions – From Entitlement to Compensation' by James Tumbridge & Ashley Roughton
'A Practical Guide to Asbestos Claims' by Jonathan Owen & Gareth McAloon

'A Practical Guide to Stamp Duty Land Tax in England and Northern Ireland' by Suzanne O'Hara
'A Practical Guide to the Law of Farming Partnerships' by Philip Whitcomb
'Covid-19, Homeworking and the Law – The Essential Guide to Employment and GDPR Issues' by Forbes Solicitors
'Covid-19 and Criminal Law – The Essential Guide' by Ramya Nagesh
'Covid-19 and Family Law in England and Wales – The Essential Guide' by Safda Mahmood
'A Practical Guide to the Law of Unlawful Eviction and Harassment – 2nd Edition' by Stephanie Lovegrove
'Covid-19, Brexit and the Law of Commercial Leases – The Essential Guide' by Mark Shelton
'A Practical Guide to Costs in Personal Injury Claims – 2nd Edition' by Matthew Hoe
'A Practical Guide to the General Data Protection Regulation (GDPR) – 2nd Edition' by Keith Markham
'Ellis on Credit Hire – Sixth Edition' by Aidan Ellis & Tim Kevan
'A Practical Guide to Working with Litigants in Person and McKenzie Friends in Family Cases' by Stuart Barlow
'Protecting Unregistered Brands: A Practical Guide to the Law of Passing Off' by Lorna Brazell
'A Practical Guide to Secondary Liability and Joint Enterprise Post-Jogee' by Joanne Cecil & James Mehigan
'A Practical Guide to the Pre-Action RTA Claims Protocol for Personal Injury Lawyers' by Antonia Ford
'A Practical Guide to Neighbour Disputes and the Law' by Alexander Walsh
'A Practical Guide to Forfeiture of Leases' by Mark Shelton
'A Practical Guide to Coercive Control for Legal Practitioners and Victims' by Rachel Horman
'A Practical Guide to the Law of Driverless Cars – Second Edition' by Alex Glassbrook, Emma Northey & Scarlett Milligan
'A Practical Guide to TOLATA Claims' by Greg Williams
'A Practical Guide to Elderly Law – 2nd Edition' by Justin Patten
'A Practical Guide to Responding to Housing Disrepair and Unfitness Claims' by Iain Wightwick

'A Practical Guide to the Law of Bullying and Harassment in the Workplace' by Philip Hyland
'How to Be a Freelance Solicitor: A Practical Guide to the SRA-Regulated Freelance Solicitor Model' by Paul Bennett
'A Practical Guide to Prison Injury Claims' by Malcolm Johnson
'A Practical Guide to the Small Claims Track – 2nd Edition' by Dominic Bright
'A Practical Guide to Advising Clients at the Police Station' by Colin Stephen McKeown-Beaumont
'A Practical Guide to Antisocial Behaviour Injunctions' by Iain Wightwick
'Practical Mediation: A Guide for Mediators, Advocates, Advisers, Lawyers, and Students in Civil, Commercial, Business, Property, Workplace, and Employment Cases' by Jonathan Dingle with John Sephton
'The Mini-Pupillage Workbook' by David Boyle
'A Practical Guide to Crofting Law' by Brian Inkster
'A Practical Guide to the Law of Domain Names and Cybersquatting' by Andrew Clemson
'A Practical Guide to the Law of Gender Pay Gap Reporting' by Harini Iyengar
'NHS Whistleblowing and the Law' by Joseph England
'Employment Law and the Gig Economy' by Nigel Mackay & Annie Powell
'A Practical Guide to Noise Induced Hearing Loss (NIHL) Claims' by Andrew Mckie, Ian Skeate, Gareth McAloon
'An Introduction to Beauty Negligence Claims – A Practical Guide for the Personal Injury Practitioner' by Greg Almond
'Intercompany Agreements for Transfer Pricing Compliance' by Paul Sutton
'Zen and the Art of Mediation' by Martin Plowman
'A Practical Guide to the SRA Principles, Individual and Law Firm Codes of Conduct 2019 – What Every Law Firm Needs to Know' by Paul Bennett
'A Practical Guide to Adoption for Family Lawyers' by Graham Pegg
'A Practical Guide to Industrial Disease Claims' by Andrew Mckie & Ian Skeate
'A Practical Guide to Conducting a Sheriff Court Proof' by Andrew Stevenson
'A Practical Guide to Vicarious Liability' by Mariel Irvine
'A Practical Guide to Applications for Landlord's Consent and Variation of Leases' by Mark Shelton
'A Practical Guide to Relief from Sanctions Post-Mitchell and Denton' by Peter Causton

'A Practical Guide to Equity Release for Advisors' by Paul Sams
'A Practical Guide to Financial Services Claims' by Chris Hegarty
'The Law of Houses in Multiple Occupation: A Practical Guide to HMO Proceedings' by Julian Hunt
'Occupiers, Highways and Defective Premises Claims: A Practical Guide Post-Jackson – 2nd Edition' by Andrew Mckie
'A Practical Guide to Financial Ombudsman Service Claims' by Adam Temple & Robert Scrivenor
'A Practical Guide to Running Housing Disrepair and Cavity Wall Claims: 2nd Edition' by Andrew Mckie & Ian Skeate
'A Practical Guide to Holiday Sickness Claims – 2nd Edition' by Andrew Mckie & Ian Skeate
'Arguments and Tactics for Personal Injury and Clinical Negligence Claims' by Dorian Williams
'A Practical Guide to Drone Law' by Rufus Ballaster, Andrew Firman, Eleanor Clot
'A Practical Guide to Compliance for Personal Injury Firms Working With Claims Management Companies' by Paul Bennett
'RTA Allegations of Fraud in a Post-Jackson Era: The Handbook – 2nd Edition' by Andrew Mckie
'RTA Personal Injury Claims: A Practical Guide Post-Jackson' by Andrew Mckie
'On Experts: CPR35 for Lawyers and Experts' by David Boyle
'An Introduction to Personal Injury Law' by David Boyle

These books and more are available to order online direct from the publisher at www.lawbriefpublishing.com, where you can also read free sample chapters. For any queries, contact us on 0844 587 2383 or mail@lawbriefpublishing.com.

Our books are also usually in stock at www.amazon.co.uk with free next day delivery for Prime members, and at good legal bookshops such as Wildy & Sons.

We are regularly launching new books in our series of practical day-to-day practitioners' guides. Visit our website and join our free newsletter to be kept informed and to receive special offers, free chapters, etc.

You can also follow us on Twitter at www.twitter.com/lawbriefpub.

www.ingramcontent.com/pod-product-compliance
Lightning Source LLC
LaVergne TN
LVHW022057200926
848481LV00003B/962